Amy Walsh & Janine Burke

# Colorful Quilts
## FOR FABRIC LOVERS

10 Easy-to-Make Projects
with a Modern Edge

From Blue Underground Studios

C&T PUBLISHING

Text and Artwork copyright © 2011 by Amy Walsh and Janine Burke

Photography and Artwork copyright © 2011 by C&T Publishing, Inc.

Publisher: Amy Marson

Creative Director: Gailen Runge

Acquisitions Editor: Susanne Woods

Editor: Lynn Koolish

Technical Editor: Susan Nelsen

Cover Designer: Kristen Yenche

Book Designer: Kerry Graham

Production Coordinator: Jenny Leicester

Production Editor: Alice Mace Nakanishi

Illustrators: Amy Walsh and Kirstie Pettersen

Photography by Christina Carty-Francis and Diane Pedersen of C&T Publishing, Inc., unless otherwise noted

Published by C&T Publishing, Inc., P.O. Box 1456, Lafayette, CA 94549

Library of Congress Cataloging-in-Publication Data

Walsh, Amy (Amy Simpson)

 Colorful quilts for fabric lovers : easy-to-make projects with a modern edge / Amy Walsh and Janine Burke.

 p. cm.

 ISBN 978-1-60705-270-8 (soft cover)

1. Patchwork quilts. 2. Quilting--Patterns. I. Burke, Janine. II. Title.

 TT835.W33733 2011

 746.46--dc22

                              2011007724

Printed in China

10 9 8 7 6 5 4 3 2 1

# Dedications

To Sophie: Heartfelt thanks for many patient hours sewing.
    —*Amy*

To Nonnie: For all your time spent patiently showing me what to do with a needle and thread.
    —*Janine*

# Acknowledgments

Thank you to our families for putting up with countless hours of sewing, typing, driving, editing, and the like. And for your loving support and care for Maggie Rose—Mom and Dad, Matthew, Anna, Mary, Stephanie, Joe, Katie, and Margaret—we could not have done it without you!

Thanks to Linnea, Stephanie, and Karen for watching Maggie and running errands.

Sean Walsh, thanks for everything—really, everything!

Jeanette, we love you!

Thanks to Patched Works, Inc.; Providence Longarm Quilting; and Brandi Frey of Quiltiste.

Thanks to Nancy and Deb for the beautiful bindings.

Special thanks to the C&T publishing team, especially Susanne Woods, Cynthia Bix, and Lynn Koolish.

Thanks to Bill and Weeks—you've inspired us both.

# CONTENTS

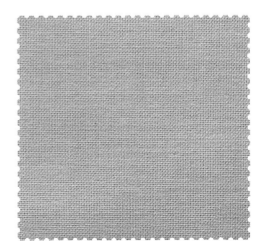

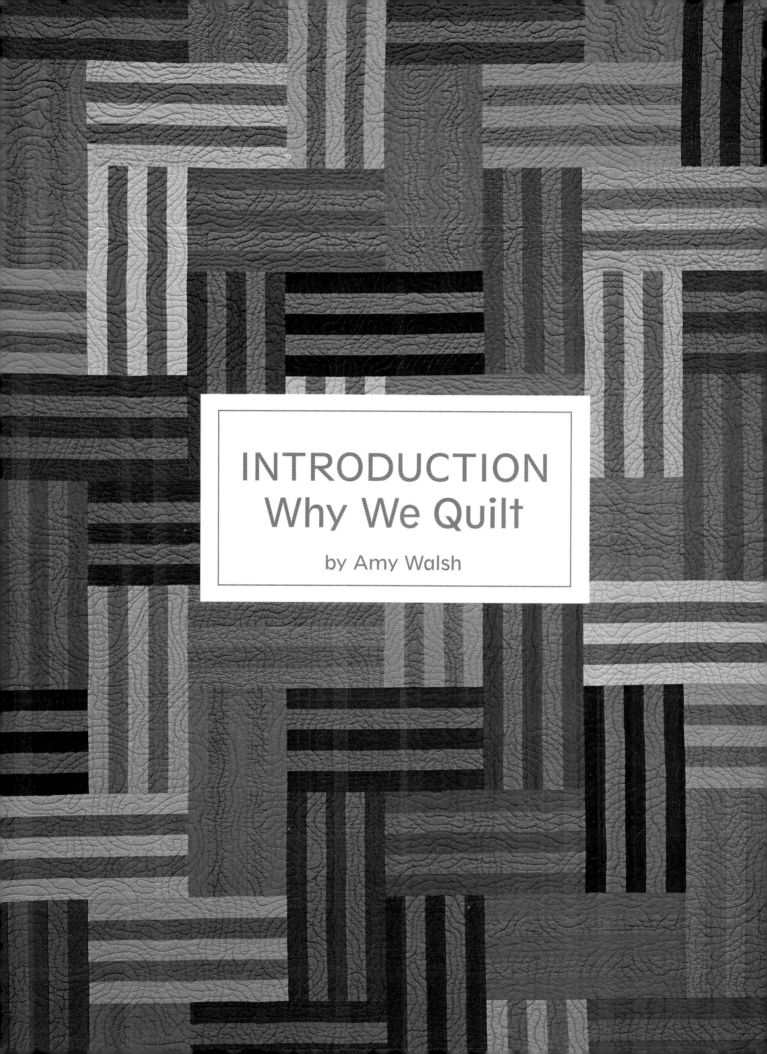

# INTRODUCTION
## Why We Quilt

by Amy Walsh

Few things are as exciting as a trip to the fabric shop. There's something about the anticipation, the smell of the fiber that hits you on the way in the door, and the first collection you see when you arrive that gets your heart pounding with possibilities. Meandering around the shop with little on your mind besides taking yards of it all home, you examine each end of the bolt carefully, being seduced by some of them enough to actually pull them out to get their full effect. You make selections and stack them on the cutting counter, placing a marker on your pile and watching it like a hawk so no one gets to it before you do. And finally, you decide how much of each fabric you will take home with you. Sometimes, the thought of missing out on a particular fabric is so terrifying that you buy the rest of the bolt! After your purchase, you hurry back to your car, only to take out your precious stack and go through it again, soaking in all of the color combinations and patterns one more time. I have been known to look through fat quarter bundles at stoplights! And, I find that at times, having new fabrics in the car can be more distracting to me than talking on my cell phone.

This may sound a little dramatic, but I love fabric so much that I don't even care if I sew it—I just want to have it, to live with it. Of course, I enjoy the process of putting a quilt together, but it's because it involves being with the fabrics. That is why I like quilts with so many different prints. At Blue Underground Studios, we like to call these *fabric lovers' quilts* (another name for *scrappy*). As we are cutting and piecing and ironing, we can reacquaint ourselves with all of the fabrics we are using. The more fabrics, the more fun!

This is the driving passion behind the patterns of Blue Underground Studios. We love designs that are relatively simple, often using basic squares and rectangles. We like to combine the fabrics that lured us into a work of beauty, while maintaining their individuality. It is in this spirit that we present these designs to you.

# GENERAL INFORMATION

## Collecting Fabrics

There is a real value in building a good stash of quality fabric. First of all, trends in fabric change all the time. Colors and styles are constantly evolving. So, when you find a print you love, don't be afraid to buy it. Amy often buys the rest of the bolt if she thinks a fabric is disappearing. However, you may want to consider your storage options before you adopt this policy. If certain shades and colors are your favorites, you might be able to find them one year and not the next. Fabric availability varies according to colors and genres currently in style. We often add fabrics from our stashes to new collections we have purchased. We have found that older fabrics add something to fabrics found in newer collections. That said, we are also proponents of weeding out our fabric collections regularly. As your styles and tastes change, so will your fabric-buying habits. Take stock of what you have so as to keep your stash balanced. If you have fabrics you are not going to use, your local shop or guild will be happy to help you find a new home for them. Many worthwhile causes are always in need of fabric donations. And, don't forget your quilting friends whose taste may be different from yours. Friends' studios are almost always a good place to de-stash.

We are frequently asked how much fabric we buy when we shop. The question of how much of a particular fabric to buy is very personal. Typically, we will buy a half-yard cut if we are stash building or collecting fabrics for a future project. A half-yard cut will give you a couple of different options when you are cutting up your fabric for a quilt (or quilts). If we *really* love a print, we will buy two or three yards. If we are choosing a focus fabric, we will buy five or six yards, depending on the size quilt we would like to make. In general, we always buy more fabric than we think we will need. Fabric emergencies are a real event—the minute you start looking for a fabric you have run out of is the precise moment it will be gone or, if you are lucky, on back order. Err on the side of caution. A penny saved is a yard lost!

Sometimes, fabric availability guides our decision about how much to purchase. For example, saturated yellow batiks are difficult to find in any quantity at one time. As we have learned this, we have started buying one-yard increments. This ensures that we will always have it when we need it. Blue and white fabrics are an example of a type of printed fabric that is not always available. If you can identify these types of fabrics within your own stash, you can fill these gaps when the opportunity arises.

Invariably, color will also be a big factor in determining your stash. If you are unsure of your favorite color, organize your fabrics and you will probably find it. For both of us, this has been a lesson well learned. We have fine-tuned our buying habits to include colors outside of our favorites, so that we have colors available to us when we go to start a project. This is not an easy thing to do, as color is an emotional thing. We used to gravitate to, and subsequently purchase, more of one color than others, resulting in a stash that was not well balanced. It truly does take work and discipline to have a stash that is usable, well-rounded, and representative of the color wheel.

Because of our love of fabric, we buy with a "don't hold back" approach. With that in mind, there are some things you might want to think about when purchasing fabric, such as, how much storage room do you have? We have known quilters to get pretty creative when it comes to storing (or hiding) fabrics. When it comes to your stash, any empty space is fair game. A well-balanced stash can actually be a source of inspiration. Having fabrics at the ready when you are will increase your productivity.

# Choosing Fabrics

We generally have an idea of the way we want a quilt to look before we make it, which makes choosing fabrics easier than going in without a plan. But sometimes, not having a plan is fun too. It's kind of like the old question "Which came first: the chicken or the egg?" Sometimes great designs start with just that—a great design. Since we work primarily with squares and rectangles, we are pretty confident that our patterns will look good in any fabrics or any collection of fabrics. Because we are fabri-holics, most of our quilts do start with the fabric. We are drawn to a particular print or grouping and then choose an appropriate design.

## Batiks

Put any balanced collection of batiks together with or without a specific color palette, and they'll look great by the very nature of the fact that they're all batiks. If you choose to do so, you can also fine-tune your batik selection by narrowing the palette, such as in *Crossroads* (page 38) or *Deco* (page 33), or limiting the fabrics to a specific degree of tone or saturation, such as in *Too Flat* (page 46) or *Slide Show* (page 59). *Too Flat* uses a variety of batiks that are mostly muted, with the addition of a sparkling cranberry and purple that pop next to the gray-based batiks. *Slide Show* uses many of the same colors as *Too Flat*, but the degree of saturation is more intense. We also like to vary the textures when choosing a batik palette. Different textures can add depth and interest to a batik quilt.

# SATURATED BATIKS OF DIFFERENT COLORS

# BLUE/GREEN COLOR PALETTE

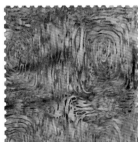

# MUTED BLUES, GREENS, AND PLUMS

## Solids

Solids are an appropriate choice for any of the quilts in this book. Choosing to work with solid fabrics ups the ante for any quilter because solids make the color and design choices more important than the fabric itself. Don't overlook them while fabric shopping. We know they don't lure you as a batik or even a Westminster print would. In fact, we've heard them referred to as "plain Janes." When you sew with solids, it's kind of an ultimate showcase for all of the aspects of quiltmaking, from the piecing to the quilting.

Most quilters think solids are very simple fabrics, but they're really a great way to improve your skills as a quilter. They can help you develop a sense of color theory, expose your weaknesses in piecing, and explore your favorite quilting techniques. Any quilting that's done on a solid is blatantly obvious. Four of the quilts in this book were made only with solids: *Snaps* (page 19), *LOFT* (page 24), *Union Station* (page 42), and *Club Noir* (page 55). We've had students who have said, "If you've seen one solid quilt, you've seen them all," or, "All-solid quilts look Amish." We couldn't agree less! The specific color palettes of these four solid quilts give each of them a different look. And, the color palettes are completely interchangeable.

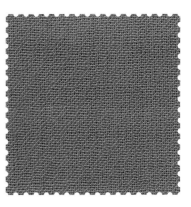

## Print Fabrics

Print fabrics are the most prevalent fabrics available to quilters. We do love working with them, and we've found we usually like to work with multiple fabric lines within one quilt. There are many ways to go about choosing a group of print fabrics to work with:

- Pick one fabric that you absolutely love, and then begin to find fabrics that go along with it. See Work with a Focus Fabric (page 17).

- Choose print fabrics by color. If you know you want to work with reds or blues, start collecting prints that fit that color scheme. Fabric selection can also be a lesson in color theory. Quite often, print fabrics will fit into many different color categories. You will find that many prints include complementary and contrasting colors, making them more interesting.

- Use a line of fabrics specifically designed to coordinate. Most fabric lines will include prints of multiple textures and designs. Varying texture in your quilts is as important as choosing colors. As with batiks, different textures can add depth and interest to finished quilts.

# VARIETY OF PRINT FABRICS

## Mavericks

We would be remiss if we didn't talk about maverick fabrics in this section. At Blue Underground Studios, maverick fabrics are those unorthodox or loner fabrics in our collection that we just had to buy, but they do not necessarily fit in with any of our current projects. Over the years we have found that these fabrics often become a focus fabric in a quilt, and the coordinating prints are chosen around it. If you do choose to throw a maverick fabric into a quilt, you will most likely find that it adds a spark of interest that was previously lacking. The prints themselves, in our definition, are typically large, bold, and unpredictable. Our favorite maverick fabric manufacturer is Alexander Henry, but we also like Westminster prints for their flamboyancy.

## Thinking outside the box: Noncotton quilting fabrics

Don't feel you have to limit yourself to conventional cotton quilting fabrics. Shirtings, poplins, dupioni and Thai silks, woolens, and even some polyester blends can also be suitable for quilting projects. In the last several years we have developed a fondness for silk. Despite the fray (which takes a little patience to work around), silk acts very much like batik. Because of the fray, we encourage you to stick with the basic shapes—squares and rectangles—while working with silk. Any of the quilts in the book would lend themselves to using silk. Additionally, old ties and garments can make interesting additions to cotton quilts. Mix it up. You might be surprised at the results.

Whatever your choice of fabrics, be sure that you love the fabrics you work with. If you're passionate about your quilting, there's no reason to quilt with fabrics you are not passionate about. Quilt fabric is readily available from a variety of sources. We've listed a few of our favorites in Favorite Resources (page 70).

# Working on a Design Wall

Whether or not you have a dedicated sewing space in your house, it is helpful to have a place to arrange your quilt before you sew the blocks together. The obvious choice for this is a design wall. You can construct your own design wall very easily by attaching a piece of batting to a large wall space if you have one available. If this is not an option, purchase a portable design wall or construct your own using flannel sheets and foam core. Use a staple gun or thumbtacks to fasten the sheets to the foam core. These makeshift design walls are easily dismantled. As a last resort, use the floor. We lay out blocks days before we have to sew them together. This allows us to make changes in block placement so we can be certain that colors and fabrics are distributed evenly.

# Washing Fabrics

Washing your fabrics is a matter of personal preference in most cases. We usually don't prewash our cotton prints simply because of the time it takes. However, we always wash batiks because of the wax used in their production process. Sometimes this residue can build up on your needle while sewing or quilting, leading to tension problems. We have found that laundered batiks are almost always easier to work with. We also wash most of the solids that we work with to ensure that they are colorfast. We recommend washing solids with Retayne, a chemical fixative for commercial fabrics, available at most quilt shops or online.

In some cases (such as when we're working with many half-yard pieces), we have found washing to be more time efficient than ironing, if ironing is required prior to cutting. What works well for us is to damp-dry the pieces and then layer them flat on top of each other (on carpet) to dry the rest of the way. The weight will flatten out the fabrics, and you will be left with pieces that are ready to cut. We generally do this the day before we need them so they have time to dry overnight.

If we use 108″-wide backing fabric, whether it's a cotton print or batik, we wash it before we use it. The very nature of its size causes it to shrink and skew differently than normal 44″–45″ fabrics.

Don't launder your fabrics with commercial laundry detergent! Detergents are harsh and create wear and bleeding before you've even started your quilt. We recommend Orvus Quilt Soap.

# Washing Quilts

We wash all of our cotton quilts after they are bound. Washing gives our quilts the "shrinky" look that we love, in addition to taking out all of the chemicals that may be in the fabrics from the production process. Use a mild soap, such as Orvus Quilt Soap—never a detergent. Wash quilts on the gentlest cycle possible. We usually dry quilts on the lowest setting and take them out of the dryer before they are completely dry.

We intend for the quilts we make to be used. We mention this because to be *used* means the quilts will also be washed. We don't want those to whom we give quilts to be afraid to wash them.

We have found that color is not only what draws people to quilt, but it's also what prevents quilters from delving into a new project. In many cases this is because of a lack of confidence. When we teach workshops, we frequently hear our students express fear of choosing fabric combinations. What we hear most often is a love of a particular fabric, but an inability to translate that love into an entire quilt. Putting fabrics and colors together can be challenging, but anyone can do it with the right tools.

If color is an area in which you're struggling, take some time to get acquainted with it. Take a trip to a nearby art museum. Which paintings are you drawn to? Why? Look in your closet. What colors do you tend to wear most? You can even try a nonquilting project that uses color to try and discover your color sense. Repaint a room in your house or change the color scheme of a room using different accent pieces.

## Color Basics

We can get you started right here with some color terminology: The three primary colors are red, blue, and yellow. When you look at a color wheel, between the primary colors are the secondary colors of orange, green, and violet. Taking this one step further, between the primary and secondary colors are the tertiary colors such as yellow-green and blue-green. Each color on the color wheel can have many shades and tints. Understanding basic color terminology can help you identify color harmonies in everyday life, as well as in your quilting life.

Colors can also be classified as cool or warm. Cool colors include blues, teals, grays, and sometimes purples and greens and are often associated with feelings of calmness and tranquility. Cool colors often are called receding colors because they tend to melt into the background when used with warm colors.

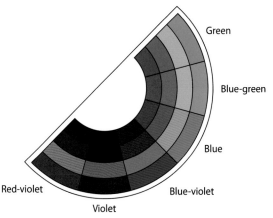

Cool colors

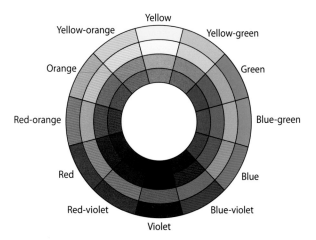

Color wheel

Warm colors include reds, oranges, and yellows and are often associated with feelings of energy and passion. Warm colors are often called advancing colors because they tend to pop out when used with cool colors. Yes, colors evoke emotion and are very personal. Your quilts will reflect your emotional reactions to color.

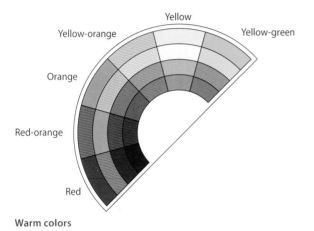

**Warm colors**

Now to the fun stuff. Knowing your way around the color wheel can help you make design decisions in quilting. There are many different ways to fine-tune a palette. If you are looking for a subtle look in a quilt, you may consider using an analogous palette—colors that are next to each other on the color wheel. Some of our favorite analogous combinations are yellow-green, green, and blue-green, and also blue-green, blue, and blue-violet.

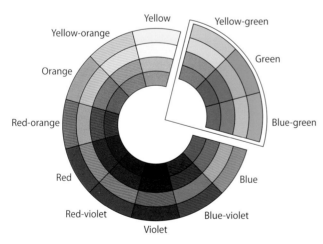

**Analogous colors**

If a subtle quilt is not what you are looking for, you may want to opt for a complementary color scheme. Complementary colors are those that are across from one another on the color wheel such as yellow-green and fuchsia, or teal and red. When you are assembling a fabric palette, you will often find yourself bending the color palette "rules," and that's okay!

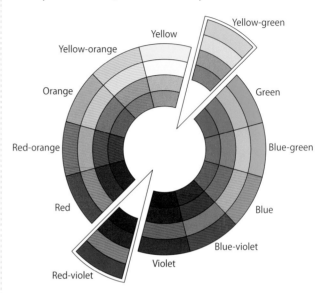

**Complementary colors**

Color theory in quilting, then, is learning how to combine colors to achieve the look you want. If you are a beginning quilter, you may want to start by choosing a favorite printed fabric and finding prints that coordinate. If you are drawn to a particular printed fabric, it probably has something to do with a color or color combination that speaks to you. Use the following guidelines in choosing coordinating and complementing prints.

### Work with a Focus Fabric

Finding prints that include similar colors and/or color values is called working with a focus fabric. For example, *Lake Shore Drive* (page 29) uses a Rowan print called Targets as the focus fabric. From this fabric, Amy pulled out periwinkle, lavender, teal, white, linen, blue, cornflower blue, sky blue, and gray. The surprise colors in this print are the lavender and linen hues. Don't be afraid to include surprise colors in your quilts. They can turn an ordinary color palette into an extraordinary one! Designers and manufacturers are well versed in color combinations. You can usually trust where their color sense will take you.

Focus fabric and related prints

### Don't Underestimate the Importance of Using a Variety of Textures in a Quilt Top

Look for stripes, dots, mottled florals, geometrics, vintage/reproductions, and novelty fabrics that will look good with your focus fabric. These prints can add different tones and shades to your quilt as well as change the look and feel of the finished project.

### Have Extra Fabrics on Hand

It's easier to remove fabrics from a selection than to get to the sewing point and find that you are lacking. Invariably, a print or two will not play well with the others. If you are not satisfied with how your fabrics look together, remove the offenders. Add them to your stash for later use.

At Blue Underground Studios, we love the look of quilts that use fabrics from more than one line or manufacturer. We encourage you to challenge yourself to work outside of a single collection. With few exceptions, colors and styles will be more varied in multiple lines and you can create a depth of color that you cannot often achieve using solely one line of fabric.

When you are comfortable working with color, solids and noncotton quilting fabrics are great tools for increasing your color skills. A wide variety of good-quality solid fabrics is available to quilters today. One of our favorite manufacturers of solids is Robert Kaufman, partly because of the sheer number of colors they offer. Dupioni silks also act like solids but have a rich sheen to them. Both are good options for those who want to flex their color muscles.

Practice is important. The time you spend making small quilts or working on projects that never come into fruition is *not* a waste. You are always learning something, even if that something teaches you what you *don't* want to do or color combinations you *don't* like. You

may not be physically logging the information for future use, but you are assimilating it into your bank of color knowledge. Also keep in mind that your tastes will change as you become a more seasoned quilter.

## The Power of the Seam

Another important element of a successful color palette is what we refer to as "the power of the seam." Two fabrics that are stitched together can look very different from the way they look when they are just lying next to each other on the design wall. Whenever you're in doubt, sew a seam. You'll be pleasantly surprised with the results.

All this having been said, color is extremely personal. There are no quilting police; and the quilts you make are a reflection of you, your tastes, and your experiences. There are good color combinations and better color combinations, but no wrong combinations. Be brave, ruthless, and even a little rebellious in your exploration of color. You won't regret any time spent building your color skills.

by Amy Walsh, 75″ × 91″

 SNAPS

My grandmother, who taught me how to sew, loved to eat licorice—especially snaps, which we would buy for her in a cellophane bag from Walgreens. I always loved the bright colors of these little candies—which inspired me to make this quilt—but did not appreciate their taste until I was an adult. Because I'm such a fan of squares, I love altering the Square-in-a-Square block to achieve different looks. Here, alternating a variation of this pattern with black solid yields a striking contemporary quilt.

## MATERIALS

*The following yardage makes a twin-size quilt. Refer to the Snaps chart (page 22) for alternate sizes and yardage requirements.*

**Assorted bright solids:** 25 strips 5½˝ × 42˝ or 4 yards total

**Solid black:** 3½ yards for block centers and alternate blocks

**Binding:** ¾ yard

**Backing:** 5¾ yards

**Batting:** 85˝ × 101˝

### TIP

To get the color variation that I wanted, I used 24 different solids in my version of *Snaps*. I made quite a few extra blocks so that I would have a lot of options when putting the quilt together.

### TIP

Don't forget to wash your solids with Retayne (pages 15 and 70), especially if you are using black!

## CUTTING

### From the assorted bright solids, cut:

■ 25 strips 5½˝ × 42˝

Cut each 5½˝ strip into:

   8 rectangles 3¼˝ × 5½˝ (Unit C)

   4 rectangles 2˝ × 5½˝; subcut into 8 rectangles 2˝ × 2¼˝ (Unit B)

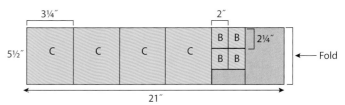

Cutting diagram

### From the black solid, cut:

■ 14 strips 7½˝ × 42˝

Cut each 7½˝ strip into:

   7 rectangles 5½˝ × 7½˝ (alternate setting blocks)

■ 5 strips 2˝ × 42˝

Cut each 2˝ strip into:

   20 squares 2˝ × 2˝ (Unit A)

# Piecing and Pressing

*Snaps* is constructed with 2 different units: the pieced blocks with black centers and the alternate black blocks. For the pictured quilt, you will need 97 pieced blocks and 98 alternate blocks.

## Making the Pieced Blocks

*Each* Snaps *block uses 2 each of Units B and C from a bright solid and 1 Unit A in black solid.*

**1.** Sew 2 B Units to either side of an A Unit. Press the seams open.

**2.** Sew 2 C Units to either side of the completed A/B Unit. Press the seams open.

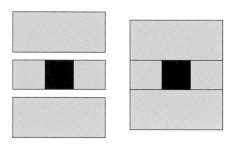

**3.** Make a total of 97 pieced blocks.

## TIP

**Be sure that your blocks measure 5½″ × 7½″. If they do not, you may have trouble when you are sewing your quilt top together.**

# Quilt Top Construction

When you have completed the pieced blocks, arrange them with the black alternate blocks in 13 rows of 15 blocks each. Refer to the Quilt Assembly Diagram as needed. Balance the color throughout so that your eye is constantly moving. When you find an arrangement you like, sew the blocks together in rows, pressing the seams open. Then sew the rows together, pressing the seams open as you sew.

Quilt Assembly Diagram

# Finishing

Refer to Quiltmaking Basics (pages 64–69) to layer, quilt, and bind your quilt.

I usually want the piecing to be the star of my quilts, not the quilting. With that in mind, I generally favor a dense, allover quilting pattern as opposed to using specific quilting designs or thread in certain areas. *Snaps* is quilted in black thread with a dense circular design that reminds me of candy. The quilting adds texture but does not distract from the piecing or the strong contrast of the colorful solids against the black.

*Snaps* has a straight-grain binding, attached by machine and finished by hand. I chose a black solid because a color would have been distracting. Sometimes solid black is the perfect way to frame a finished quilt top.

*Snaps* quilting

# ■ *Snaps* Alternate Sizing ■

Four alternate sizes are given for Snaps in this chart. Follow the cutting instructions for the individual strips (page 20).

| | BLOCK SET | TOTAL PIECED BLOCKS | TOTAL ALTERNATE BLOCKS | BRIGHT SOLIDS | BLACK | BACKING | BATTING | BINDING |
|---|---|---|---|---|---|---|---|---|
| **BABY** 35˝ × 35˝ | 7 × 5 | 17<br>Unit A: 17<br>Unit B: 34<br>Unit C: 34 | 18 | 1 yard, cut into 5 strips 5½˝ × 42˝ | 1 yard, cut into 3 strips 7½˝ × 42˝ and 1 strip 2˝ × 42˝ | 2½ yards | 45˝ × 45˝ | ⅓ yard |
| **THROW** 55˝ × 63˝ | 11 × 9 | 49<br>Unit A: 49<br>Unit B: 98<br>Unit C: 98 | 50 | 2¼ yards, cut into 13 strips 5½˝ × 42˝ | 2¼ yards, cut into 8 strips 7½˝ × 42˝ and 3 strips 2˝ × 42˝ | 3¾ yards | 65˝ × 73˝ | ½ yard |
| **QUEEN** 85˝ × 91˝ | 17 × 13 | 110<br>Unit A: 110<br>Unit B: 220<br>Unit C: 220 | 111 | 4½ yards, cut into 28 strips 5½˝ × 42˝ | 4 yards, cut into 16 strips 7½˝ × 42˝ and 6 strips 2˝ × 42˝ | 9 yards | 95˝ × 101˝ | ¾ yard |
| **KING** 105˝ × 119˝ | 21 × 17 | 178<br>Unit A: 178<br>Unit B: 356<br>Unit C: 356 | 179 | 7¼ yards, cut into 45 strips 5½˝ × 42˝ | 6¼ yards, cut into 26 strips 7½˝ × 42˝ and 9 strips 2˝ × 42˝ | 9¾ yards | 115˝ × 129˝ | 1 yard |

# ■ Alternate Colorways and Sizes ■

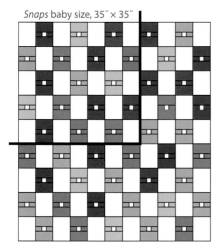

*Snaps* baby size, 35″ × 35″

*Snaps* throw size, 55″ × 63″

*Snaps* queen size, 85″ × 91″

*Snaps* king size, 105″ × 119″

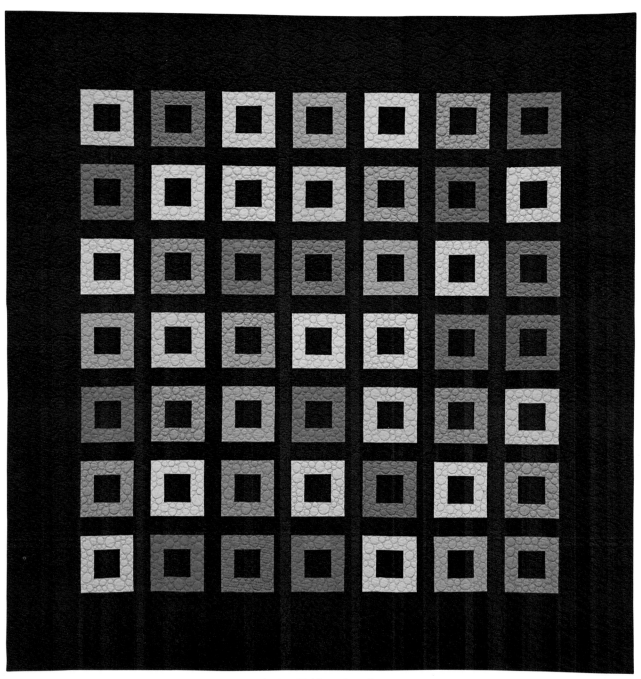

by Amy Walsh, , 70″ × 70″

LOFT

I have always wanted to live in a loft in downtown Chicago. I love the idea of escaping the frenetic energy of the streets in a cool, industrial-feeling apartment that overlooks our beautiful city. This is the type of quilt that would fit in perfectly with my idea of the perfect interior of such a home.

**FINISHED BLOCK:**
6˝ × 6˝

**FINISHED QUILT:**
70˝ × 70˝

# MATERIALS

*The following yardage makes a throw-sized quilt. Refer to the LOFT chart (page 27) for alternate sizes and yardage requirements.*

**Assorted pastel solids:** 10 strips 6½˝ × 42˝ or 2 yards total

**Solid gray:** 5 yards for block centers, sashing, and outside borders

**Binding:** ½ yard

**Backing:** 5½ yards

**Batting:** 80˝ × 80˝

> **TIP**
> Don't forget to wash your solids with Retayne (pages 15 and 70)!

# CUTTING

## From the assorted pastels, cut:

- **10 strips 6½˝ × 42˝**

Cut each 6½˝ strip into:

  10 rectangles 2˝ × 6½˝ (Unit C)

  10 rectangles 2˝ × 3½˝ (Unit B)

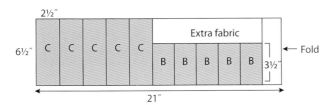

Cutting diagram

> **TIP**
> Each 6½˝ strip will yield enough frames for 5 *LOFT* blocks.

## From the solid gray, cut:

- **3 strips 6½˝ × 42˝**

Cut each 6½˝ strip into:

  16 rectangles 2½˝ × 6½˝ (vertical sashing)

- **5 strips 3½˝ × 42˝**

Cut each 3½˝ strip into:

  11 squares 3½˝ × 3½˝ (Unit A)

## From the remaining gray fabric, cut:

- **1¾-yards' length and a 2¼-yards' length**

Make the following subcuts *parallel to the selvage* of each of these pieces:

  6 strips 2½˝ × 1¾ yards (horizontal sashing)

  *Note: We recommend waiting until you have sewn the blocks together in rows to cut these strips to the exact length.*

  4 strips 8½˝ × 2¼ yards (outer borders)

  *Note: We recommend waiting until you have sewn the inner blocks together to cut the border strips to the exact length.*

# Piecing and Pressing

To make the pictured quilt, you will need to piece 49 *LOFT* blocks. You will use only 42 vertical sashing pieces.

## Making the pieced blocks

*Note: Each* LOFT *block uses 2 B and 2 C Units in the same color solid and 1 A Unit.*

**1.** Sew 2 B Units to either side of an A Unit. Press the seams open.

**2.** Sew 2 C Units to either side of the completed A/B Unit. Press the seams open.

**3.** Make a total of 49 pieced blocks.

# Quilt Top Construction

**1.** When you have completed your pieced blocks, arrange them with the gray vertical sashing units and horizontal untrimmed sashing strips between blocks. Refer to the Quilt Assembly Diagram as needed. To make the pictured quilt, you will need 7 rows, each with 7 blocks. Balance the color throughout so that your eye is constantly moving. When you find an arrangement you like, sew the blocks together with the vertical sashing to make 7 horizontal rows. Press the seams open as you sew.

**2.** Measure some of the rows to help you determine the length to cut your horizontal sashing strips. If all of your cutting and ¼″ seams are accurate, the finished length of the rows should be 54½″.

**3.** Trim the horizontal sashing strips to the appropriate length, and sew the rows together with the sashing in between. Press the seams open as you sew.

**4.** Measure the length and the width through the center of the quilt top to determine the length of the borders. If all of your cutting and ¼″ seams are accurate, the side borders should measure 8½″ × 54½″. The top and bottom borders should measure 8½″ × 70½″. Cut the border strips to the appropriate measurements. Add the side borders first, pressing the seams open. Then add the top and bottom borders, pressing the seams open. The quilt top should measure 70½″ × 70½″.

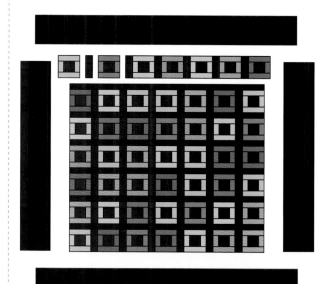

Quilt Assembly Diagram

# Finishing

Refer to Quiltmaking Basics (pages 64–69) to layer, quilt, and bind your quilt.

I usually want the piecing to be the star of my quilts—not the quilting. However, I felt that *LOFT* was an exception to this rule and had it custom quilted with two shades of gray thread. The quilting in the dark gray field is in a shade of gray that is almost invisible on the fabric. I wanted the background to have a lot of texture but did not want the thread to be at all visible. The pastel frames are quilted in a pale shade of gray thread. As in the background, I did not want the quilting to be too distracting. The design in both the background and the frames is geometric and contemporary looking—very fitting for this type of quilt.

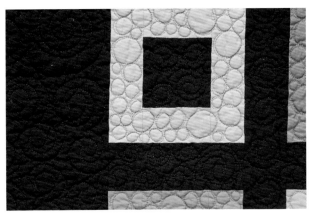
*LOFT* quilting

*LOFT* has a straight-grain binding, attached by machine and finished by hand. I chose to use the border and background fabric for the binding of this quilt. I did not want the binding to frame the quilt. Instead, I wanted the binding to melt into the quilt and disappear.

# ▪ *LOFT* Alternate Sizing ▪

Four alternate sizes for *LOFT* are given in this chart. The gray yardages include enough yardage to cut the sashing and border strips from the selvage edge. Follow the cutting instructions for the 3½″ and 6½″ strips (pages 25).

| | BLOCK SET | TOTAL BLOCKS | ASSORTED PASTEL SOLIDS | SOLID GRAY | BACKING | BATTING | BINDING |
|---|---|---|---|---|---|---|---|
| **BABY** 46″ × 46″ | 4 × 4 | 16<br>Unit A: 16<br>Unit B: 32<br>Unit C: 32 | 1 yard, cut into 4 strips 6½″ × 42″ | 3 yards, cut into 1 strip 6½″ × 42″ and 2 strips 3½″ × 42″. From the lengthwise grain cut 2 strips 8½″ × 46½″, 2 strips 8½″ × 30½″, and 3 strips 2½″ × 30½″. | 3¼ yards | 56″ × 56″ | ½ yard |
| **FULL** 78″ × 78″ | 8 × 8 | 64<br>Unit A: 64<br>Unit B: 128<br>Unit C: 128 | 2½ yards, cut into 13 strips 6½″ × 42″ | 5¾ yards, cut into 4 strips 6½″ × 42″ and 6 strips 3½″ × 42″. From the lengthwise grain cut 2 strips 8½″ × 78½″, 2 strips 8½″ × 62½″, and 7 strips 2½″ × 62½″. | 5 yards | 88″ × 88″ | ¾ yard |
| **QUEEN** 94″ × 94″ | 10 × 10 | 100<br>Unit A: 100<br>Unit B: 200<br>Unit C: 200 | 4 yards, cut into 20 strips 6½″ × 42″ | 7¼ yards, cut into 6 strips 6½″ × 42″ and 10 strips 3½″ × 42″. From the lengthwise grain cut 2 strips 8½″ × 94½″, 2 strips 8½″ × 78½″, and 9 strips 2½″ × 78½″. | 9 yards | 104″ × 104″ | ¾ yard |
| **KING** 118″ × 118″ | 13 × 13 | 169<br>Unit A: 169<br>Unit B: 338<br>Unit C: 338 | 6½ yards, cut into 34 strips 6½″ × 42″ | 10 yards, cut into 10 strips 6½″ × 42″ and 16 strips 3½″ × 42″. From the lengthwise grain cut 2 strips 8½″ × 118½″, 2 strips 8½″ × 102½″, and 12 strips 2½″ × 102½″. | 10¾ yards | 128″ × 128″ | 1 yard |

# ▪ Alternate Colorways and Sizes ▪

You can drastically change the look of *LOFT* by changing the color palette. And, although we love the look of this quilt in solids, it would look equally stunning in batiks or your favorite prints. We have included some colorways you might like to experiment with.

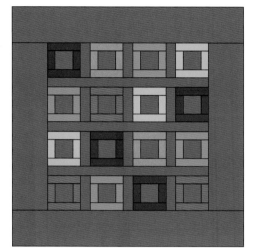

*LOFT* baby size, 46″ × 46″

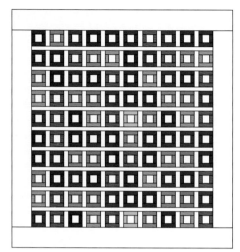

*LOFT* queen size, 94″ × 94″

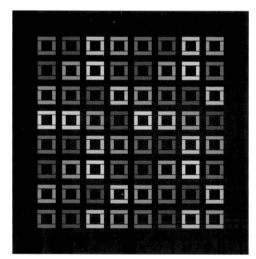

*LOFT* full size, 78″ × 78″

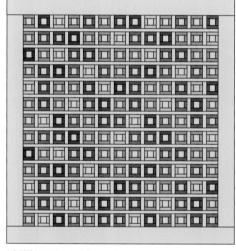

*LOFT* king size, 118″ × 118″

by Amy Walsh, 57″ × 72″

# LAKE SHORE DRIVE

Anyone who knows me knows how much I love, love, love Chicago. One of my favorite drives to take in the city is down Lake Shore Drive, especially on a sunny day. Lake Michigan is on one side and the beautiful skyline is on the other. This particular color palette is my picture of Lake Shore Drive on a clear winter day. The different shades of blue suggest the sky and frozen water, as does the addition of white.

## MATERIALS

*The following yardage makes a twin-size quilt. Refer to the* Lake Shore Drive *chart (page 32) for alternate sizes and yardage requirements.*

**Assorted coordinating small-scale prints:** 20 strips 3˝ × 42˝ **or** 1¾ yards total for pieced 4-patch blocks

**Large-scale print:** 2¼ yards for the alternate 8½˝ strips

**Binding:** ½ yard

**Backing:** 3¾ yards

**Batting:** 67˝ × 82˝

### TIP

This quilt is perfect for any of the larger prints you want to work with—especially those that you love too much to cut up. Choose prints for the pieced blocks that match the colors in your alternate print. And, as always, the more prints the better. We used about 30 for the pictured quilt.

## CUTTING

**From the assorted coordinating small-scale prints, cut:**

- 20 strips 3˝ × 42˝

Cut each 3˝ strip into:

8 rectangles 3˝ × 5˝

**From the large-scale print, cut:**

- 4 strips 8½˝ × length of fabric (parallel to the selvage). *Note: These strips will be trimmed to fit later.*

## Piecing and Pressing

Each *Lake Shore Drive* block is essentially a Four-Patch constructed with 2 rectangles from 2 different fabrics. You can change the way this quilt looks by piecing your rectangles from 4 different fabrics, giving the quilt a scrappier look.

**1.** Sew 2 sets of 2 rectangles together. Press the seams open as you sew.

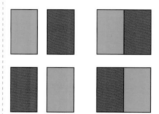

**2.** Sew the resulting 2 units together. Press the seams open.

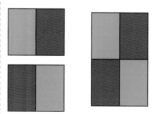

**3.** Make a total of 40 Four-Patch blocks to make the pictured quilt.

### TIP

Be sure that your blocks measure 5½˝ × 9½˝. If they do not, you might have trouble when you are sewing your quilt top together.

## Quilt Top Construction

When you have completed the blocks, arrange them in 5 rows alternating with the 8½˝ strips. Each row should have 8 Four-Patch blocks. Refer to the Quilt Assembly Diagram as needed. When you find an arrangement you like, sew the Four-Patch blocks together in vertical rows and measure the length of the four-patch rows. Trim the 8½˝ strips to that length. Then sew all rows together, pressing the seams open as you sew.

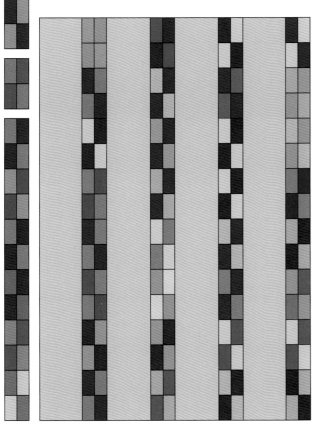

Quilt Assembly Diagram

## Finishing

Refer to Quiltmaking Basics (pages 64–69) to layer, quilt, and bind your quilt.

Because the fabrics used here are so busy, *Lake Shore Drive* is quilted in a light gray thread with an allover cloudlike pattern. However, based on the fabric you choose for your alternate fabric, you might decide that a different quilting pattern or thread color is just what your quilt needs.

I used straight-grain binding, attached by machine and finished by hand. Again, I have used the same print as the alternate large strips for the binding. This is a distinct design decision, and the binding almost melts into the quilt.

*Lake Shore Drive* quilting

# *Lake Shore Drive* Alternate Sizing ■

Two alternate sizes for *Lake Shore Drive* are given in this chart. The large-scale print yardages include enough yardage to cut the 8½″ alternate strips parallel to the selvage. Follow the cutting instructions for the individual strips (page 30).

| | FOUR-PATCH ROWS | FOUR-PATCH BLOCKS | ALTERNATE LARGE-SCALE FABRIC | ASSORTED SMALL-SCALE PRINTS | BATTING | BACKING | BINDING |
|---|---|---|---|---|---|---|---|
| BABY/WALL 31″ × 45″ | 3 | 15 | 1½ yards, cut into 2 strips 8½″ × 45½″ | ¾ yard, cut into 8 strips 3″ × 42″ | 43″ × 55″ | 1½ yards | ⅜ yard |
| QUEEN 83″ × 99″ | 7 | 77 | 5¾ yards, cut into 6 strips 8½″ × 99½″ | 3½ yards, cut into 39 strips 3″ × 42″ | 93″ × 109″ | 7¾ yards | ¾ yard |

# ■ Alternate Colorways and Sizes ■

*Lake Shore Drive* baby/wall size, 31″ × 45″

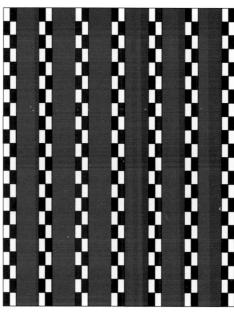

*Lake Shore Drive* queen size, 83″ × 99″

by Amy Walsh, 78″ × 78″

DECO

I came across this simple little pattern one day while tooling around the streets of downtown Milwaukee with my sisters. This brick inlay was on the side of an old public school building we drove by. I of course immediately hauled out a napkin from the bottom of my purse and furiously began to sketch it out—an action that nets me no end of laughter from my loving siblings. And here it is, years later, as one of our favorite patterns. This quilt literally lends itself to any color palette that you may be hankering to work with. The bright blue squares can be subtle or contrasting—either looks smashing. Here is a perfect opportunity to haul out your stash and see what inspires you!

# MATERIALS

*The following yardage makes a full-size quilt. Refer to the Deco chart (page 36) for alternate sizes and yardage requirements.*

**Assorted green, gray, and taupe batiks:** 33 strips 6½″ × 42″ **or** 6¼ yards total

**Blue or teal batik:** 6 strips 2½″ × 42″ **or** ½ yard

**Backing:** 5 yards

**Binding:** ¾ yard

**Batting:** 88″ × 88″

## TIP

One of the keys to a successful *Deco* quilt is a variety of fabrics. Here, I have used about 40 assorted shades of green and gray—one of the benefits to having a good fabric stash. When you are looking for a wide range of fabrics in a particular palette, it is often hard to find them all in one shopping trip.

# CUTTING

## From the assorted green, gray, and taupe batiks, cut:

- **33 strips 6½″ × 42″**

Cut each 6½″ strip into:

13 rectangles 2½″ × 6½″ (Unit C)

Trim strip to 4½″ to cut 3 rectangles 2½″ × 4½″ (Unit B).

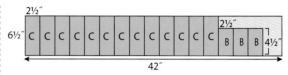

Cutting diagram

*Note: You will have some extra B and C Units left at the end of your piecing.*

## From the blue and teal batiks, cut:

- **6 strips 2½″ × 42″**

Cut each 2½″ strip into:

16 squares 2½″ × 2½″ (Unit A)

## SIDEBAR

I intentionally did not construct this quilt using strata or strip set units. I have found that I much prefer the more varied look you can achieve by piecing the individual blocks. However, if you prefer to use stratas, cut the number of strips needed for the quilt size you want to make, and sew them together in sets of three. Cut them into 6½″ × 6½″ squares for the Rail Fence blocks.

# Piecing and Pressing

*Deco* is composed of 2 different blocks: the plain Rail Fence blocks and the Deco blocks. You will need a total of 84 Rail Fence blocks and 85 Deco blocks to make the pictured quilt.

## Rail Fence Block Construction

Each Rail Fence block requires 3 C Units from different fabrics. Sew all 3 units together, pressing the seams open. Make a total of 84 blocks.

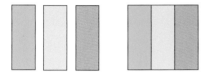

## Deco Block Construction

Each Deco block requires 1 A Unit, 1 B Unit, and 2 C Units from different fabrics. Sew the A Unit to the B Unit. Press the seams open. Sew the 2 C Units to opposite sides of the A/B Unit. Press the seams open. Make a total of 85 Deco blocks.

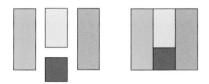

## TIP

Be sure that your blocks measure 6½˝ × 6½˝. If they do not, you might have trouble when you are sewing your quilt top together.

## Quilt Top Construction

Arrange the blocks in 13 rows of 13 blocks each, alternating A and B Blocks. Refer to the Quilt Assembly Diagram as needed. When you find an arrangement you like, sew the blocks together in rows, pressing the seams open as you sew. Sew the rows together, pressing the seams open.

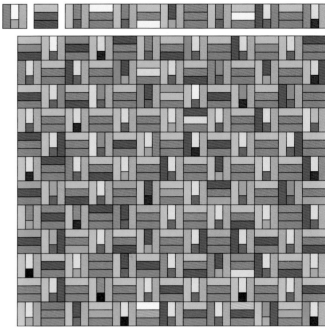

Quilt Assembly Diagram

## Finishing

Refer to Quiltmaking Basics (pages 64–69) to layer, quilt, and bind your quilt.

*Deco* is quilted with a dense, allover swirl design. I chose swirls for two reasons: The first is that I liked the closeness of the lines in this design. Dense quilting can make a great quilt greater—especially after it is washed. I also liked the way the swirls continue the *Deco* theme I have going in this quilt. Whenever possible, we try to connect the quilting to the larger design idea in our quilts.

I selected a very neutral green thread to quilt *Deco*—it almost melts into the fabric. It adds a lot of texture without detracting from the graphic nature of the piecing. *Deco* has a straight-grain binding attached by machine and finished by hand.

*Deco* quilting

# ▪ *Deco* Alternate Sizing ▪

Four alternate sizes for *Deco* are given in this chart. Follow the cutting instructions for the individual strips (page 34).

| | BLOCK SET | RAIL FENCE BLOCKS | DECO BLOCKS | GREEN/GRAY | BLUE/TEAL | BACKING | BATTING | BINDING |
|---|---|---|---|---|---|---|---|---|
| BABY/WALL 42˝ × 42˝ | 7 × 7 | 24<br><br>Unit C: 72 | 25<br><br>Unit A: 25<br>Unit B: 25<br>Unit C: 50 | 2 yards, cut into 10 strips 6½˝ × 42˝ | ¼ yard, cut into 2 strips 2½˝ × 42˝ | 3 yards | 52˝ × 52˝ | ½ yard |
| THROW 54˝ × 54˝ | 9 × 9 | 40<br><br>Unit C: 120 | 41<br><br>Unit A: 41<br>Unit B: 41<br>Unit C: 82 | 3¼ yards, cut into 16 strips 6½˝ × 42˝ | ½ yard, cut into 3 strips 2½˝ × 42˝ | 3½ yards | 64˝ × 64˝ | ½ yard |
| QUEEN 90˝ × 90˝ | 15 × 15 | 112<br><br>Unit C: 336 | 113<br><br>Unit A: 113<br>Unit B: 113<br>Unit C: 226 | 8¼ yards, cut into 44 strips 6½˝ × 42˝ | ¾ yard, cut into 8 strips 2½˝ × 42˝ | 8½ yards | 100˝ × 100˝ | ¾ yard |
| KING 114˝ × 114˝ | 19 × 19 | 180<br><br>Unit C: 540 | 181<br><br>Unit A: 181<br>Unit B 181<br>Unit C: 362 | 10½ yards, cut into 56 strips 6½˝ × 42˝ | 1 yard, cut into 12 strips 2½˝ × 42˝ | 10½ yards | 124˝ × 124˝ | 1 yard |

# ▪ Alternate Colorways and Sizes ▪

*Deco* baby/wall size, 42″ × 42″

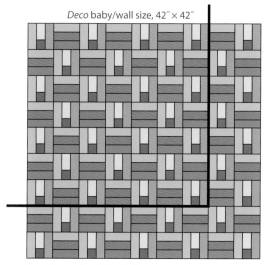

*Deco* throw size, 54″ × 54″

*Deco* queen size, 90″ × 90″

*Deco* king size, 114″ × 114″

Varying the design size and the texture of the batiks will add interest to your finished quilt.

by Amy Walsh, 84˝ × 84˝

# CROSSROADS

After green, blue is definitely my favorite color. An old project I started in a design class inspired me to use this collection of batiks, all of which are blue or relatives of blue. I love the way these fabrics go together. Finishing this quilt made me want to try it in other analogous palettes.

# MATERIALS

*The following yardage makes a queen-size quilt. Refer to the Crossroads chart (page 41) for alternate sizes and yardage requirements.*

**Assorted blue and green batiks:** 40 strips 6½″ × 42″ **or** 7½ yards total **or** 33 fat quarters

**Backing:** 8 yards

**Binding:** ¾ yard

**Batting:** 94″ × 94″

## TIP

I used more than 40 different fabrics in the *Crossroads* quilt to get the look and texture that I wanted. The more fabrics, the better! Dig into your stash to find your most interesting batiks. If you are lacking, ask a quilting friend—or better yet, go shopping!

# CUTTING

*Crossroads is made up of 3 different blocks. You can make subtle changes to the look of this quilt by altering the number of each block you include. We made an equal number of all 3 blocks, interspersing them randomly throughout the quilt.*

## TIP

Cut and sew together a few of your blocks so you can see what they look like before you cut all of your fabrics. You may find that you like the look of Block A better than Block B. Or you might decide to add or remove some of your fabrics. You might end up saving time and fabric this way!

Cut the assorted batiks into 40 strips 6½″ × 42″. Each 6½″ × 42″ strip will yield enough pieces for 5 *Crossroads* blocks. Each fat quarter yields 6 blocks. Decide how many of each block you want, and cut accordingly—you will need 196 blocks to make the pictured quilt. Block unit measurements are given below:

### Block A

1 rectangle 4¾″ × 6½″ (side unit)

1 rectangle 1″ × 6½″ (center unit)

1 rectangle 1¾″ × 6½″ (side unit)

### Block B

1 rectangle 3¾″ × 6½″ (side unit)

1 rectangle 1″ × 6½″ (center unit)

1 rectangle 2¾″ × 6½″ (side unit)

### Block C

2 rectangles 3¼″ × 6½″ (side units)

1 rectangle 1″ × 6½″ (center unit)

# Piecing and Pressing

Refer to the block diagrams to arrange each block. The 3 *Crossroads* blocks are constructed in the same way: Sew 2 side units of fabric 1 to the center unit of fabric 2, pressing seams open as you sew. Each block should measure 6½″ × 6½″.

# Quilt Top Construction

Arrange the blocks in 14 rows of 14 blocks each. Refer to the Quilt Assembly Diagram as needed. Balance the different shades and textures throughout so that your eye is constantly moving across the quilt top. When you find an arrangement you like, sew the blocks together in rows, pressing seams open as you sew. Then sew the rows together, pressing the seams open as you sew.

Quilt Assembly Diagram

# Finishing

Refer to Quiltmaking Basics (pages 64–69) to layer, quilt, and bind your quilt.

*Crossroads* is quilted with a dense, allover pattern in a neutral blue thread, adding texture and movement to the quilt without distracting from the piecing or the beauty of the fabrics. *Crossroads* has a straight-grain binding, attached by machine and finished by hand.

*Crossroads* quilting

The pieced backing of *Crossroads* has a maverick strip of red added.

# ■ *Crossroads* Alternate Sizing ■

Four alternate sizes are given for *Crossroads* in this chart. Follow the cutting for the individual strips (page 39).

| | BLOCK SET | TOTAL BLOCKS | ASSORTED BLUE/GREEN BATIKS | BACKING | BATTING | BINDING |
|---|---|---|---|---|---|---|
| **BABY/WALL** 36˝ × 36˝ | 6 × 6 | 36 | 1¾ yards, cut into 8 strips 6½˝ × 42˝ | 2½ yards | 46˝ × 46˝ | ⅓ yard |
| **THROW** 54˝ × 54˝ | 9 × 9 | 81 | 3¼ yards, cut into 17 strips 6½˝ × 42˝ | 3¾ yards | 64˝ × 64˝ | ½ yard |
| **TWIN/FULL** 72˝ × 72˝ | 12 × 12 | 144 | 5½ yards, cut into 29 strips 6½˝ × 42˝ | 4¾ yards | 82˝ × 82˝ | ⅔ yard |
| **KING** 102˝ × 102˝ | 17 × 17 | 289 | 10¾ yards, cut into 58 strips 6½˝ × 42˝ | 9½ yards | 112˝ × 112˝ | 1 yard |

# ■ Alternate Colorways and Sizes ■

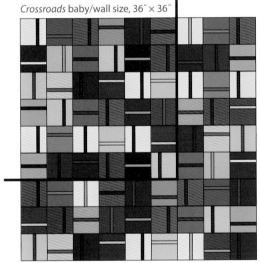

*Crossroads* baby/wall size, 36˝ × 36˝

*Crossroads* throw size, 54˝ × 54˝

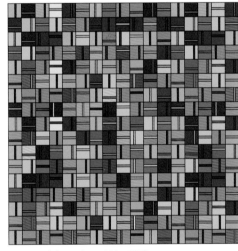

*Crossroads* king size, 102˝ × 102˝

*Crossroads* twin/full size, 72˝ × 72˝

by Janine Burke, 60″ × 82½″

# UNION STATION

Once upon a time, I used to take the train into Chicago's Union Station on my way to work in the morning and then back out again at night. The gray rails represent the train tracks (you probably figured that out), while the palette represents the multicolors of the multicultures who pass through Union Station by the thousands every day.

FINISHED SQUARE BLOCK: 7½˝ × 7½˝

FINISHED RECTANGLE BLOCK: 7½˝ × 15˝

FINISHED QUILT: 60˝ × 82½˝

## MATERIALS

*The following yardage makes a throw-size quilt. Refer to the* Union Station *chart (page 45) for alternate sizes and yardage requirements.*

**Assorted bright solids:** 20 strips 6˝ × 42˝ **or** 3½ yards total

**Gray:** 2½ yards

**Batting:** 70˝ × 92˝

**Backing:** 5¼ yards

**Binding:** ¾ yard

## CUTTING

### From each of the assorted bright solids, cut:

- **20 strips 6˝ × 42˝**

Cut each 6˝ strip into:

  3 strips 2˝ × 42˝

### From the gray, cut:

- **40 strips 2˝ × 42˝**

# Piecing and Pressing

*Union Station is constructed by making strata or strip-pieced units. You will make a total of 20 stratas, 1 with each accent color.*

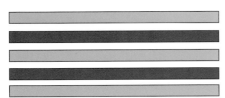

Strata of 2 gray strips between 3 accent strips

## TIP

Whenever you piece strata, first sew strips into pairs, and then sew pairs to pairs. This will help you avoid the rainbow curve effect that occurs when sewing each consecutive strip onto a growing unit. By sewing into twos, then fours, and eights, your strata will remain straight.

**1.** Sew the outer pairs together. Press the seams open.

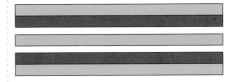

**2.** Add the middle strip. Press the seam open.

**3.** Join the units together. Press the seam open.

**4.** Measure the width of your strata. A precise ¼˝ seam will yield an 8˝ strata width.

## More Cutting

If your strata units measure 8˝, subcut 3 squares at 8˝ each and 1 rectangle at 15½˝.

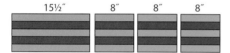

Cutting diagram

If your strata units measure something else, for example, 8¼˝, use that measurement for the 3 squares—cut your squares 8¼˝ × 8¼˝. The rectangle will be cut using the following formula:

**(strata width × 2) – ½˝ = size of rectangle to be cut**

*Example:* (8¼˝ × 2) – ½˝ = 16˝; cut rectangle 8¼˝ × 16˝.

## Quilt Top Construction

Refer to the Quilt Assembly Diagram as necessary to place the square blocks and rectangular blocks into rows. The rectangular blocks will only be placed horizontally. You will use 20 rectangular blocks. To achieve the look of the "vertical" block, match up square blocks from one row to another. To make the sample quilt, you will need 20 matching squares. You will further need 8 single squares. Two will be used in the top row, another 2 in the bottom row, another 2 in row 4, and 2 more in row 8. You'll have 12 squares left over.

Place the squares and rectangles into rows. Make sure that the colors are placed evenly throughout the quilt top so that your eye keeps moving. When you find an

arrangement you like, sew the blocks together in rows, pressing the seams open. Then sew the rows together, pressing the seams open as you sew.

Quilt Assembly Diagram

## Finishing

Refer to Quiltmaking Basics (pages 64–69) to layer, quilt, and bind your quilt.

When we work with solids, we love dense quilting to showcase both the fabric and the quilting. *Union Station* is quilted with a neutral gray thread. We used straight-grain binding, attached by machine and finished by hand.

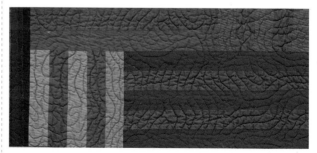

*Union Station* quilting

# ▪ *Union Station* Alternate Sizing ▪

Two alternate sizes for *Union Station* are given in this chart. Follow the cutting and strata information in the project (page 43).

| | RECTANGLES | MATCHING SQUARES | SINGLE SQUARES | ASSORTED BRIGHT SOLIDS | GRAY | BATTING | BACKING | BINDING |
|---|---|---|---|---|---|---|---|---|
| TWIN 75″ × 90″ | 27 | 5 | 10 | 4¾ yards, cut into 27 strips 6″ × 42″ | 3¼ yards, cut into 56 strips 2″ × 42″ | 85″ × 100″ | 5¾ yards | ¾ yard |
| QUEEN 90″ × 90″ | 33 | 66 | 12 | 5¾ yards, cut into 33 strips 6″ × 42″ | 3¾ yards, cut into 66 strips 2″ × 42″ | 100″ × 100″ | 8½ yards | ¾ yard |

# ▪ Alternate Colorways and Sizes ▪

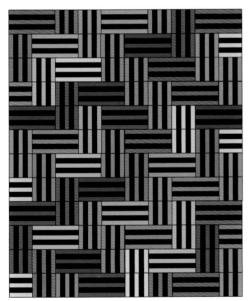

*Union Station* twin size, 75″ × 90″

*Union Station* queen size, 90″ × 90″

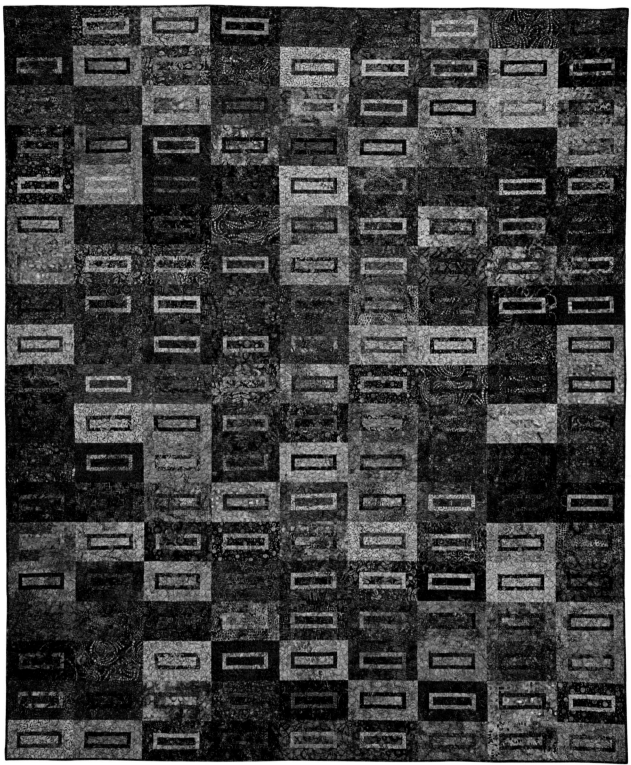

by Janine Burke, 81˝ × 95˝

# TOO FLAT

I love the architecture in Chicago. Whether it's residential or commercial, it appeals to my eye. I am frequently inspired by architecture for patterns, and this one is no exception. Playing on the phrase *two-flat* in reference to apartment-style living, *Too Flat* represents the many cozy homes throughout the city and surrounding suburbs.

**FINISHED BLOCK:**
9˝ × 5˝

**FINISHED QUILT:**
81˝ × 95˝

## MATERIALS

*The following yardage makes a queen-size quilt. Refer to the* Too Flat *chart (page 49) for alternate sizes and yardage requirements.*

**Assorted batiks:** 43 strips 8˝ × 42˝ **or** 43 fat quarters

**Binding:** ¾ yard

**Backing:** 7¾ yards

**Batting:** 91˝ × 105˝

## CUTTING

*We have included cutting instructions for both 42˝ strips as well as fat quarters.*

> ### TIP
> We encourage you to cut just 2 contrasting batiks to begin with so that you can construct a test block. This way you can verify the accuracy of your pieces and you can see how your fabrics are going together.

Each block is constructed of the following pieces:

    1 rectangle 1½˝ × 5½˝ (Unit A)

    2 rectangles 1˝ × 5½˝ (Unit B)

    2 rectangles 1˝ × 2½˝ (Unit C)

    2 rectangles 2˝ × 6½˝ (Unit D)

    2 rectangles 2˝ × 5½˝ (Unit E)

*Too Flat* block

### From the assorted batiks, cut:

- **Each 8˝ strip into 4 strips 2˝ × 42˝**

Cut each 2˝ strip into:

    2 rectangles 2˝ × 6½˝ (Unit D)

    2 rectangles 2˝ × 5½˝ (Unit E)

    1 rectangle 1½˝ × 5½˝ (Unit A)

    2 rectangles 1˝ × 5½˝ (Unit B)

    2 rectangles 1˝ × 2½˝ (Unit C)

Cutting diagram for each 2˝ strip

> ### TIP
> One 2˝ strip yields the pieces needed to make 1 block; 4 strips will yield 4 blocks.

### Or from each of the 43 fat quarters, see cutting diagram (page 48) to cut:

- **4 strips 2˝ × 21˝**

Subcut each strip into 2 rectangles 2˝ × 6½˝ (Unit D) and 1 rectangle 2˝ × 5½˝ (Unit E).

- **1 strip 2˝ × 21˝**

Subcut into 3 rectangles 2˝ × 5½˝ (Unit E) and 2 rectangles 1˝ × 2½˝ (Unit C).

- **1 strip 2˝ × 21˝**

Subcut into 1 rectangle 2˝ × 5½˝ (Unit E), 1 rectangle 1½˝ × 5½˝ (Unit A), and 6 rectangles 1˝ × 2½˝ (Unit C).

- **1 strip 1½˝ × 21˝**

Subcut into 3 rectangles 1½˝ × 5½˝ (Unit A).

- **3 strips 1˝ × 21˝**

Subcut into 8 rectangles 1˝ × 5½˝ (Unit B).

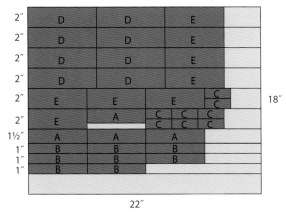

Cutting diagram for each fat quarter

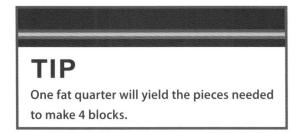

## TIP

**One fat quarter will yield the pieces needed to make 4 blocks.**

## Piecing and Pressing

*Too Flat* blocks are constructed of 2 contrasting prints. From fabric 1 you will need A, D, and E Units. From fabric 2 you will need B and C Units.

**1.** Sew 2 B Units to either side of the A Unit. Press the seams open.

**2.** Add the C Units onto the ends of the A/B Unit. Press the seams open.

**3.** Add the D Units to the A/B/C Unit. Press the seams open.

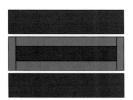

**4.** Add the E Units. Press the seams open. Your block should measure 9½″ × 5½″.

## Quilt Top Construction

When you have completed the pieced blocks, arrange them in 19 rows of 9 blocks. Refer to the Quilt Assembly Diagram as needed. Balance the color throughout so that your eye is constantly moving. When you find an arrangement you like, sew the blocks together in rows, pressing the seams open. Then sew the rows together, pressing the seams open as you sew.

Quilt Assembly Diagram

# Finishing

Refer to Quiltmaking Basics (pages 64–69) to layer, quilt, and bind your quilt.

*Too Flat* is quilted with a dense, allover stone pattern using a neutral gray thread, adding to the texture of the quilt without detracting from the palette. I used Hobbs wool batting to further enhance the texture of the quilt after it is laundered. I used straight-grain binding, attached by machine and finished by hand.

*Too Flat* quilting

Pieced backing of *Too Flat*

## ■ *Too Flat* Alternate Sizing ■

This chart gives four alternate sizes for *Too Flat*. Follow the cutting instructions for the 8″ × 42″ strips or the fat quarters (page 47).

| | BLOCK SET | TOTAL BLOCKS | ASSORTED BATIKS | BATTING | BACKING | BINDING |
|---|---|---|---|---|---|---|
| **BABY/WALL** 45″ × 45″ | 5 × 9 | 45 | 12 fat quarters **or** 12 strips 8″ × 42″ | 55″ × 55″ | 3 yards | ⅜ yard |
| **LAP** 54″ × 70″ | 6 × 14 | 84 | 21 fat quarters **or** 21 strips 8″ × 42″ | 64″ × 80″ | 3⅝ yards | ½ yard |
| **THROW** 63″ × 80″ | 7 × 16 | 112 | 28 fat quarters **or** 28 strips 8″ × 42″ | 73″ × 90″ | 5 yards | ⅝ yard |
| **TWIN** 72″ × 90″ | 8 × 18 | 144 | 36 fat quarters **or** 36 strips 8″ × 42″ | 82″ × 100″ | 5¾ yards | ¾ yard |

# ▪ Alternate Colorways and Sizes ▪

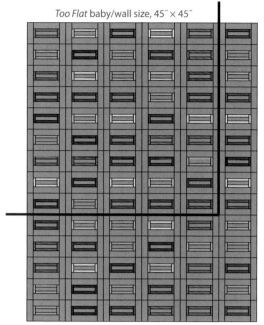

*Too Flat* baby/wall size, 45″ × 45″

*Too Flat* lap size, 54″ × 70″

*Too Flat* throw size, 63″ × 80″

*Too Flat* twin size, 72″ × 90″

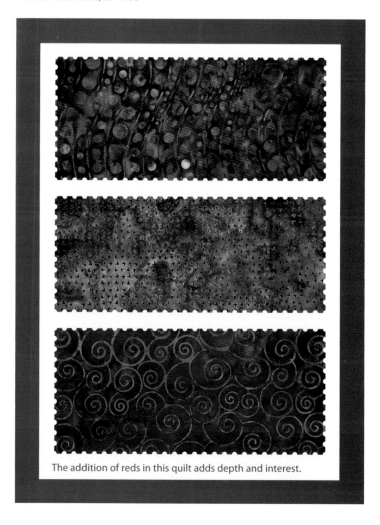

The addition of reds in this quilt adds depth and interest.

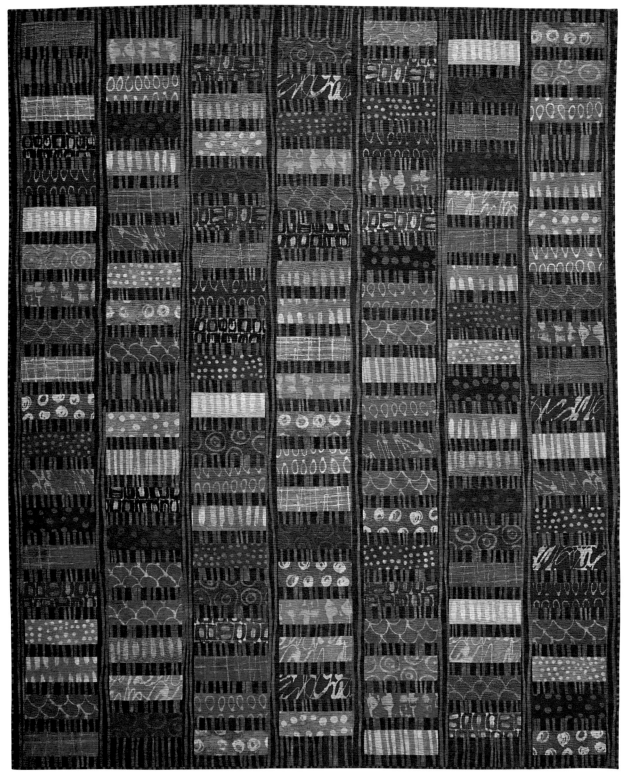

by Janine Burke, 75″ × 91½″

# HIGH RISE

**FINISHED QUILT:**
75˝ × 91½˝

The lines and geometry of buildings are aesthetically pleasing to me. They intrigue me at night when random lights are on inside but the shadows of the night wrap themselves around the outside. I chose this darker palette to emulate that warm, shadowy feel. I hope you enjoy the simple piecing of this quilt and hope you, too, come to look at buildings with a different eye.

# MATERIALS

*The following yardage makes a twin-size quilt. Refer to the High Rise chart (page 54) for alternate sizes and yardage requirements.*

**Assorted prints:** 35 strips 3½˝ × 42˝ **or** 3½ yards total

**Dark print:** 3½ yards for the background

**Binding:** ¾ yard

**Backing:** 5¾ yards

**Batting:** 85˝ × 102˝

# CUTTING

**From the assorted prints, cut:**

- **35 strips 3½˝ × 42˝**

**From the background, cut:**

- **2 strips 4¼˝ × 42˝**

Cut each 4¼˝ strip into:

    6 rectangles 4¼˝ × 9½˝
    (for the top and bottom of columns 2, 4, and 6)

- **55 strips 2˝ × 42˝**

Cut only 1 strip into:

    4 rectangles 2˝ × 9½˝ (for the pieces
    on the bottom of columns 1, 3, 5, and 7)

# Piecing and Pressing

*High Rise* is constructed using a piecing technique known as strata or strip piecing.

**1.** Sew each of the 35 assorted 3½˝ strips to a 2˝ background strip. These will make up 35 strata units. Press the seams open. Each 2-strip strata should measure 5˝ × 42˝.

**2.** Cut each strata into 4 rectangles 9½˝ × 5˝.

9½˝

# Quilt Top Construction

At this point, you have 140 rectangles 9½˝ × 5˝, but you will only use 137 rectangles in the final layout. Refer to the Quilt Assembly Diagram (next page) to help you arrange the blocks.

**1.** On a design space such as a wall or the floor, arrange the rectangles into 7 columns. Keeping the background strip of each unit toward the top of the quilt, place 20 units into each of columns 1, 3, 5, and 7; and place only 19 units into each of columns 2, 4, and 6. Arrange the pieces, balancing color throughout the quilt.

**2.** Once you like your arrangement, you need to adapt the top units from columns 2, 4, and 6. Remove the background strip from each unit and replace it with a background strip 4¼˝ × 9½˝ as shown. Return these units to your layout.

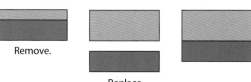

Remove.

Replace.

Top units for even columns

**3.** Now add a 2″ × 9½″ background strip to each of the bottom units in columns 1, 3, 5, and 7. Then add a 4¼″ × 9½″ background strip to the bottom units in columns 2, 4, and 6. Return these to their appropriate positions in your layout.

Bottom units for odd columns

Bottom units for even columns

**4.** You are ready to sew the units into columns. First, sew the blocks together in pairs. Then sew the pairs together. Continue sewing pairs of block units together until you have 7 finished columns.

**5.** If your seam allowance is a precise ¼″, your columns should measure 91½″ in length. Sew the remaining 2″ background strips together to make 8 strips 2″ × 91½″, and place the strips between the columns of blocks. If your columns measure something else, you will need to customize your vertical strips to fit.

**6.** Sew the columns and strips together, pressing the seams open.

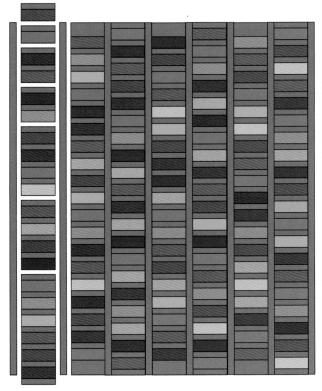

Quilt Assembly Diagram

# Finishing

Refer to Quiltmaking Basics (pages 64–69) to layer, quilt, and bind your quilt.

*High Rise* was quilted in a dense, allover water meander design with a dark olive thread. I used Hobbs wool batting, which provides that wonderful shrinky look after quilts are washed. I used straight-grain binding, attached by machine and finished by hand.

*High Rise* quilting

# ◾ *High Rise* Alternate Sizing ◾

This chart gives two alternate sizes for *High Rise*. Follow the instructions for making the strata, cutting the strips, and creating the unique top and bottom column units (page 52).

| | BLOCK SET | RECTANGLE UNITS | ASSORTED PRINTS | BACKGROUND | BATTING | BACKING | BINDING |
|---|---|---|---|---|---|---|---|
| LAP/THROW 54″ × 55½″ | 5 × 12 | 58 | 1¾ yards, cut into 15 strips 3½″ × 42″ | 1¾ yards, cut into 1 strip 4¼″ × 42″ and 25 strips 2″ × 42″ | 64″ × 66″ | 3¾ yards | ½ yard |
| QUEEN 96″ × 96″ | 9 × 21 | 185 | 4¾ yards, cut into 47 strips 3½″ × 42″ | 4½ yards, cut into 1 strip 4¼″ × 42″ and 74 strips 2″ × 42″ | 106″ × 106″ | 9 yards | 1 yard |

# ◾ Alternate Colorways and Sizes ◾

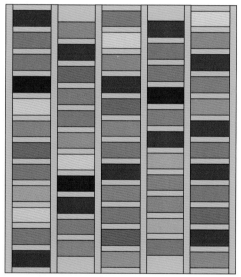

*High Rise* lap/throw size, 54″ × 55½″

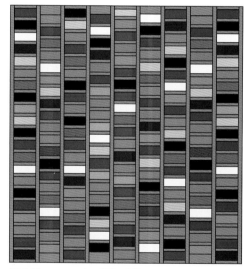

*High Rise* queen size, 96″ × 96″

by Janine Burke, 54″ × 72″

# CLUB NOIR

I've long been intrigued by the dichotomy of nightclubs—dark and sensual, yet loud and lively. This color palette was chosen to reflect that atmosphere: mysterious yet bright.

# MATERIALS

*The following yardage makes a twin-size quilt. Refer to the Club Noir chart (page 58) for alternate sizes and yardage requirements.*

**Assorted solids:** 18 strips 9˝ × 42˝ **or** 4¾ yards total **or** 20 fat quarters

**Binding:** ½ yard

**Backing:** 3¾ yards

**Batting:** 64˝ × 82˝

# CUTTING

*We have included cutting instructions for both 42˝ strips as well as fat quarters.*

**TIP**

Cut up just 2 contrasting solids to begin with so that you can construct a test block. This way you can verify the accuracy of your pieces and you can see how your fabrics are going together.

## Cutting from assorted solids

From the assorted solids, cut:

■ **18 strips 9˝ × 42˝**

Cut each 9˝ strip into:

   1 strip 4½˝ × 42˝; subcut into 3 squares 4½˝ × 4½˝, 3 rectangles 3½˝ × 4½˝, and 6 rectangles 1½˝ × 4½˝.

   3 strips 1½˝ × 42˝; subcut each strip into 2 rectangles 1½˝ × 12½˝ and 3 rectangles 1½˝ × 4½˝.

**TIP**

One 9˝ strip yields the pieces needed to make 3 blocks.

## Or cutting from fat quarters

From each fat quarter, cut:

■ **1 strip 4½˝ × 20˝**
Subcut into 3 squares 4½˝ × 4½˝ and 4 rectangles 1½˝ × 4½˝.

■ **1 strip 4½˝ × 20˝**
Subcut into 3 rectangles 3½˝ × 4½˝ and 5 rectangles 1½˝ × 4½˝.

■ **6 strips 1½˝ × 20˝**
Subcut each strip into 1 rectangle 1½˝ × 12½˝ and 1 rectangle 1½˝ × 4½˝.

**TIP**

One fat quarter will yield the pieces needed to make 3 blocks.

# Piecing and Pressing

*Club Noir* blocks are constructed of a frame solid and 3 different contrasting solids. For the frame solid you will need 2 rectangles 1½˝ × 12½˝ and 4 rectangles 1½˝ × 4½˝. From contrasting solids, you will need 1 rectangle 1½˝ × 4½˝, 1 rectangle 3½˝ × 4½˝ and 1 square 4½˝ × 4½˝. For the pictured quilt, you will need 54 blocks.

**1.** Arrange the pieces needed for each block.

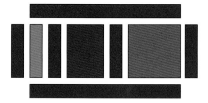

**2.** Sew the center pieces together. Press the seams open.

**3.** Add the 12½˝ rectangles to the top and bottom of the center unit. Press the seams open. Your block should measure 12½˝ × 6½˝.

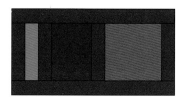

# Quilt Top Construction

Arrange the completed blocks in rows, referring to the Quilt Assembly Diagram. Balance the color throughout so that your eye is constantly moving. When you find an arrangement you like, sew the blocks together into the large 3-unit blocks, pressing the seams open. Sew the 3-unit blocks into rows, and then sew the rows together, pressing the seams open as you sew.

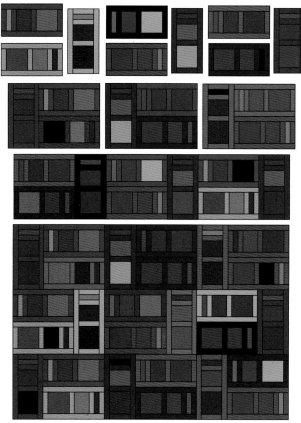

Quilt Assembly Diagram

# Finishing

Refer to Quiltmaking Basics (pages 64–69) to layer, quilt, and bind your quilt.

*Club Noir* is quilted with a dense, pointy, paisley pattern, using a dark gray thread that adds to the texture of the quilt without detracting from the dark solid palette. We really enjoy working with solids because they provide a wonderful canvas to showcase quilting with thread that matches the fabrics. Hobbs Heirloom 80/20 batting was used to give the quilt that shrinky look after washing. I used straight-grain binding, attached by machine and finished by hand.

*Club Noir* quilting

# ■ *Club Noir* Alternate Sizing ■

This chart presents *Club Noir* in two additional sizes. Follow the cutting instructions for the individual strips (page 56).

| | 3-UNIT BLOCK SET | # OF BLOCKS | ASSORTED SOLIDS | BATTING | BACKING | BINDING |
|---|---|---|---|---|---|---|
| **BABY/WALL** 36″ × 36″ | 2 × 3 | 18 | 1¾ yards, cut into 6 strips 9″ × 42″ | 46″ × 46″ | 1¼ yards | ½ yard |
| **QUEEN/KING** 108″ × 108″ | 6 × 9 | 162 | 13¾ yards, cut into 54 strips 9″ × 42″ | 118″ × 118″ | 10 yards | 1 yard |

# ■ Alternate Colorways and Sizes ■

*Club Noir* baby/wall size, 36″ × 36″

*Club Noir* queen/king size, 108″ × 108″

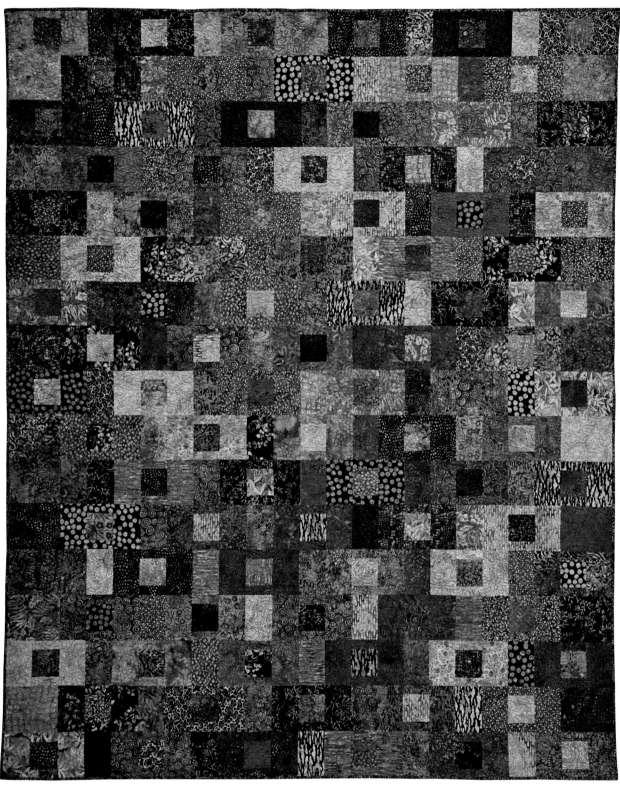

by Janine Burke, 69″ × 85″

 SLIDE SHOW

**B**ack in the "old" days, before digital cameras, we had film. From the times of silent movies, there was always film. These blocks remind me of the days of film, whether slides or reel-to-reel. So put on your favorite film, pop a bowl of popcorn, and make an evening of it!

# MATERIALS

*The following yardage makes a throw-size quilt. Refer to the Slide Show chart (page 62) for alternate sizes and yardage requirements.*

**Assorted batiks:** 33 strips 7˝ × 42˝ **or** 6¾ yards total

**Binding:** ¾ yard

**Backing:** 5½ yards

**Batting:** 79˝ × 95˝

# CUTTING

## TIP

Cut just 2 contrasting batiks to begin with so that you can construct a test block. This way you can verify the accuracy of your pieces and you can see how your fabrics are going together.

## From the assorted batiks, cut:

■ **33 strips 7˝ × 42˝**

From **16** strips, cut each 7˝ strip into:

2 rectangles 3½˝ × 7˝; subcut into 4 squares 3½˝ × 3½˝ (Unit A).

7 rectangles 3½˝ × 7˝; subcut into 7 rectangles 3½˝ × 5½˝ (Unit C) and 6 rectangles 1½˝ × 3½˝ (Unit B).

1 rectangle 5½˝ × 6½˝ (Unit D).

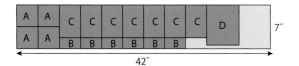

From the remaining **17** strips, cut each 7˝ strip into:

2 rectangles 3½˝ × 7˝; subcut into 4 squares 3½˝ × 3½˝ (Unit A).

9 rectangles 3½˝ × 7˝; subcut into 9 rectangles 3½˝ × 5½˝ (Unit C) and 6 rectangles 1½˝ × 3½˝ (Unit B).

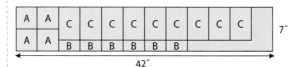

# Piecing and Pressing

Each block is constructed of the following pieces:

1 square 3½˝ × 3½˝ (Unit A)

2 rectangles 1½˝ × 3½˝ (Unit B)

2 rectangles 3½˝ × 5½˝ (Unit C)

*Slide Show* blocks are constructed of 2 contrasting prints. From fabric 1 you will need 1 A Unit and from fabric 2 you will need 2 B Units and 2 C Units. You will need 94 blocks to make the pictured quilt. The additional C Units will be used as spacers in the rows.

Sew 2 B Units to either side of the A Unit. Press the seams open. Add the C Units to the sides of the A/B Unit, pressing the seams open. The block should measure 9½˝ × 5½˝.

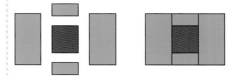

# Quilt Top Construction

1. Arrange the blocks and spacers in rows. Refer to the Quilt Assembly Diagram, as needed. Balance the color throughout so that your eye is constantly moving. Odd-numbered rows will have 6 blocks and 5 C-Unit spacers. Even-numbered rows will have 5 blocks, 4 C-Unit spacers, and 2 D-Unit spacers.

Odd rows

Even rows

2. When you find an arrangement you like, sew the blocks together in rows, pressing the seams open. Then sew the rows together, pressing the seams open as you sew.

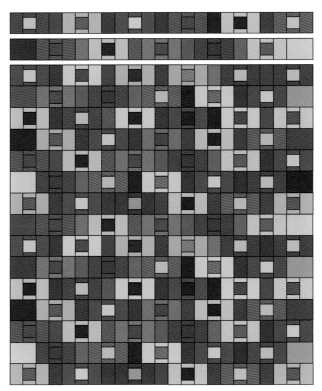

Quilt Assembly Diagram

# Finishing

Refer to Quiltmaking Basics (pages 64–69) to layer, quilt, and bind your quilt.

*Slide Show* is quilted with a dense, allover design in lime thread. I used Hobbs wool batting to give the quilt a great shrinky look after it is washed.

I used straight-grain binding, attached by machine and finished by hand.

*Slide Show* quilting

# ■ *Slide Show* Alternate Sizing ■

This chart presents *Slide Show* in two additional sizes. The strip cutting and the row construction are indicated in the chart for each size.

| | ROWS | TOTAL BLOCKS | ASSORTED BATIKS | BATTING | BACKING | BINDING |
|---|---|---|---|---|---|---|
| **LAP**<br>**57″ × 55″** | 11 | | 3¾ yards, cut into 18 strips 7″ × 42″ | | | |
| Odd rows: 5 blocks, 4 C Units<br>Even rows: 4 blocks, 3 C Units, 4 D Units | | 50 | Unit A: 50<br>Unit B: 100<br>Unit C: 119<br>Unit D: 10 | 67″ × 65″ | 4 yards | ½ yard |
| **QUEEN/KING**<br>**105″ × 105″** | 21 | | 12¼ yards, cut into 62 strips 7″ × 42″ | | | |
| Odd rows: 9 blocks, 8 C Units<br>Even rows: 8 blocks, 7 C Units, 2 D Units | | 179 | Unit A: 179<br>Unit B: 358<br>Unit C: 516<br>Unit D: 20 | 115″ × 115″ | 10 yards | 1 yard |

# ■ Alternate Colorways and Sizes ■

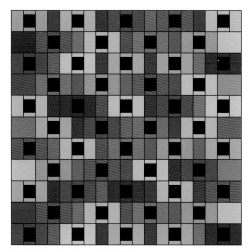

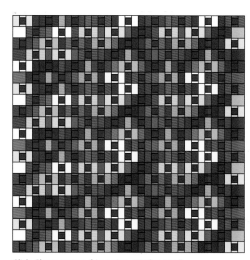

*Slide Show* lap size, 57″ × 55″

*Slide Show* queen/king size, 105″ × 105″

Pieced backing of *Slide Show*

# QUILTMAKING
# BASICS

## Seam Allowances

A ¼˝ seam allowance is used for all of the projects in this book. It's a good idea to do a test seam before you begin sewing to check that your ¼˝ seam is accurate. Accuracy is the key to successful piecing.

There is no need to backstitch. Seamlines will be crossed by another seam, which will anchor them.

## Pressing

We prefer to iron all of our seams open. If you have not tried this before, give it a shot. We love the flat, graphic nature of quilts that have absolutely flat seams. Press lightly in an up-and-down motion. Avoid using a very hot iron or overironing, which can distort shapes and blocks. We do like to use steam to iron as well.

*Note:* The only time it is not appropriate to iron seams open is when you are planning to hand quilt your top. Machine quilting will anchor flat-pressed seams, making them stand up to washing and wear.

## Borders

Whenever possible, we prefer to cut borders parallel to the selvage, using long pieces of fabric so we can avoid piecing them together. However, piecing works fine when you do not have a long-enough length of fabric.

### Butted Borders

In most cases the side borders are sewn on first. When you have finished the quilt top, measure it through the center vertically. This will be the length to cut the side borders. Place pins at the centers of all four sides of the quilt top, as well as in the center of both side border strips. Pin the side borders to the quilt top first, matching the center pins and ends. Using a ¼˝ seam allowance, sew the borders to the quilt top and press seams open.

Measure horizontally across the center of the quilt top, including the side borders. This will be the length to cut the top and bottom borders. Repeat, pinning, sewing, and pressing.

# Finishing

We recommend that you give careful consideration to all of the finishing elements of your quilt. Careful choices for batting, backing, binding, and quilting can make a good quilt top into a spectacular quilt top. Likewise, poor choices can undermine your hard work and money!

## Backing

Plan on making the backing a minimum of 10″ longer and wider than the quilt top. For *most* of the quilts in this book, you will need to piece the backing from multiple yardage lengths. Specific yardage requirements are given for each quilt. If you are sending your quilt top out to a longarm quilter to be finished, be sure you check to see what requirements the quilter may have for backing. Most quilters want extra fabric on all sides of the backing as well as a squared-up back so that they can begin working on your quilt with minimum trouble.

If you have the time, consider piecing the back from any leftover quilting fabrics or blocks in your collection. This not only can save you money but gives you the chance to customize the look of your back. Try adding fabrics that mean something to you or the recipient of your quilt. Or, add a label. These little details can add so much to your finished project.

## Batting

Consider your batting choices carefully. There are many available today. We wash almost all of our quilts after they are bound, so we choose battings that will not only stand up to multiple washings but also give an antiqued look after they are laundered. Our favorite batts are Hobbs Heirloom 80/20, Hobbs Wool, and Quilter's Dream Select Loft. Each of these batts is thin enough to use for a wallhanging and has enough drape to use in a full- or queen-size quilt.

## Layering

If you choose to quilt your top yourself and do not have a longarm machine, you will need to layer and baste your quilt carefully. Spread the backing wrong side up, and tape down the edges with masking tape. (If you are working on carpet, you can use T-pins to secure the backing to the carpet.) Center the batting on top, smoothing out any folds. Place the quilt top right side up on top of the batting and backing, making sure it is centered.

## Basting

Basting keeps the quilt sandwich layers from shifting while you are quilting.

If you plan to machine quilt, pin baste the quilt layers together with safety pins placed a minimum of 3″–4″ apart. Begin basting in the center and move toward the edges first in vertical, then horizontal, rows. Try not to pin directly on the intended quilting lines.

If you plan to hand quilt, baste the layers together with thread using a long needle and light-colored thread. Knot one end of the thread. Using stitches approximately the length of the needle, begin in the center and move out toward the edges in vertical and horizontal rows approximately 4″ apart. Add two diagonal rows of basting.

## Quilting

Quilting, whether by hand or machine, should enhance the pieced design of the quilt. All of the quilts presented in this book lend themselves well to allover, freehand, or pantograph patterns. We love the texture that allover quilting produces, especially once a quilt has been laundered. We prefer the look of very densely quilted designs that keep the eye moving across the quilt top. If you like to do your own quilting, consider trying free-motion designs such as spirals, meandering, or paisleys. If you work with a longarm quilter, pick his/her brain. Professional quilters pair designs with quilt tops for a living. Use them and their knowledge, as they are a valuable resource.

Many professional quilters have computer-guided machines. This makes dense quilting more affordable and accessible.

# Binding

Trim excess batting and backing from the quilt even with the edges of the quilt top.

## *Double-Fold Straight-Grain Binding*

For a ¼˝ finished binding, cut the binding strips 2˝ wide and piece them together with diagonal seams to make a continuous binding strip. Trim the seam allowance to ¼˝. Press the seams open.

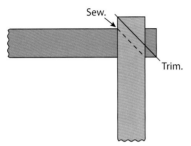

Sew from corner to corner.

Completed diagonal seam

Press the entire strip in half lengthwise with wrong sides together. With raw edges even, pin the binding to the front edge of the quilt a few inches away from the corner, and leave the first few inches of the binding unattached. Start sewing, using a ¼˝ seam allowance.

Stop ¼˝ away from the first corner (see Step 1), and backstitch 1 stitch. Lift the presser foot and needle. Rotate the quilt one-quarter turn. Fold the binding at a right angle so it extends straight above the quilt and the fold forms a 45° angle in the corner (see Step 2). Then bring the binding strip down even with the edge of the quilt (see Step 3). Begin sewing at the folded edge. Repeat in the same manner at all corners.

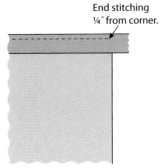

Step 1. Stitch to ¼˝ from corner.

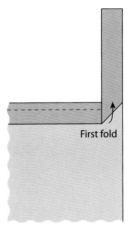

Step 2. First fold for miter

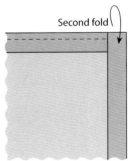

Step 3. Second fold alignment

Continue stitching until you are back near the beginning of the binding strip. See Finishing the Binding Ends for tips on finishing and hiding the raw edges of the ends of the binding.

## Continuous Bias Binding

A continuous bias involves using a square sliced in half diagonally and then sewing the triangles together so that you continuously cut marked strips to make continuous bias binding. The same instructions can be used to cut bias for piping. Cut the fabric for the bias binding or piping so it is a square. For example, cut an 18″ × 18″ square. Cut the square in half diagonally, creating 2 triangles.

Sew these triangles together as shown, using a ¼″ seam allowance. Press the seam open.

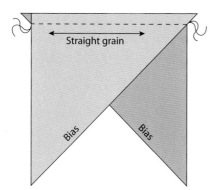

Sew triangles together.

Using a ruler, mark the parallelogram created by the 2 triangles with lines spaced the width you need to cut your bias. Cut about 5″ along the first line.

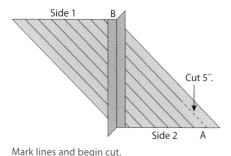

Mark lines and begin cut.

Join Side 1 and Side 2 to form a tube. The raw edge at line A will align with the raw edge at B. This will allow the first line to be offset by 1 strip width. Pin the raw edges right sides together, making sure that the lines match. Sew with a ¼″ seam allowance. Press the seam open. Cut along the drawn lines, creating a continuous strip.

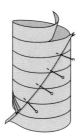

Press the entire strip in half lengthwise with wrong sides together. Place binding on quilt as described in the Double-Fold Straight-Grain Binding section.

See Finishing the Binding Ends for tips on finishing and hiding the raw edges of the ends of the binding.

# Finishing the Binding Ends

## Method 1

After stitching around the quilt, fold under the beginning tail of the binding strip ¼″ so that the raw edge will be inside the binding after it is turned to the backside of the quilt. Place the end tail of the binding strip inside the beginning folded end. Continue to attach the binding and stitch slightly beyond the starting stitches. Trim the excess binding. Fold the binding over the raw edges to the quilt back and hand stitch, mitering the corners.

## Method 2

*See our blog entry at ctpubblog.com; search for "invisible seam"; then scroll down to "Quilting Tips: Completing a Binding with an Invisible Seam."*

Fold the ending tail of the binding back on itself where it meets the beginning binding tail. From the fold, measure and mark the cut width of your binding strip. Cut the ending binding tail to this measurement. For example, if your binding is cut 2⅛″ wide, measure from the fold on the ending tail of the binding 2⅛″ and cut the binding tail to this length.

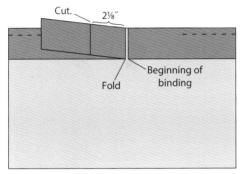

Cut binding tail.

Open both tails. Place one tail on top of the other tail at right angles, right sides together. Mark a diagonal line from corner to corner and stitch on the line. Check that you've done it correctly and that the binding fits the quilt, and then trim the seam allowance to ¼″. Press open.

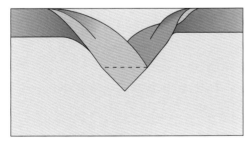

Stitch ends of binding diagonally.

Refold the binding and stitch this binding section in place on the quilt. Fold the binding over the raw edges to the quilt back and hand stitch.

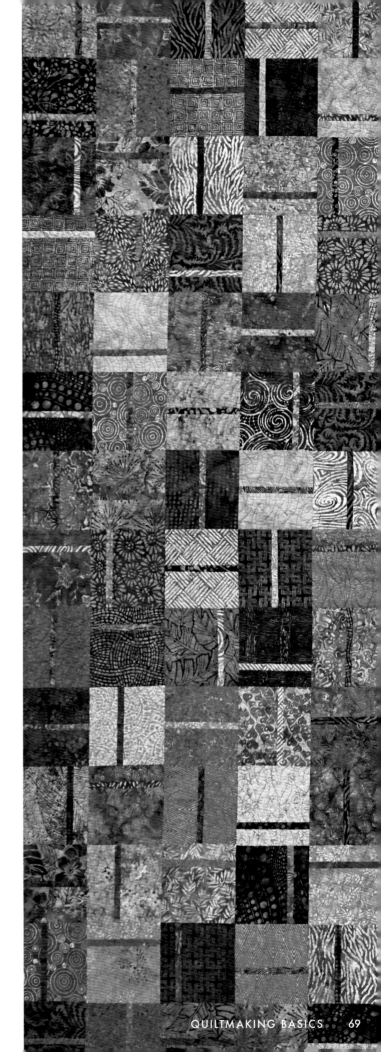

# FAVORITE RESOURCES

## General Reference

Hargrave, Harriet, *From Fiber to Fabric: The Essential Guide to Quiltmaking Textiles*. Lafayette, CA: C&T Publishing, 1997. Available as an electronic download or print on demand from www.ctpub.com.

This Is a comprehensive book and a must for all fabric-lovers' libraries.

## Books (and Tools) on Color

Barnes, Christine, *The Quilter's Color Club: Secrets of Value, Temperature & Special Effects • 12 Hands-On Exercises • 8 Projects*. Lafayette, CA: C&T Publishing, 2011.

Practical approaches for using color in quilts.

Menz, Deb, *Color Works: The Crafter's Guide to Color*. Loveland, CO: Interweave Press, 2004.

Complete information about color relationships with pages of useful tear-away swatches.

Ringle, Weeks, and Kerr, Bill, *Quiltmaker's Color Workshop: The FunQuilts' Guide to Understanding Color and Choosing Fabrics*. Minneapolis, MN: Rockport Publishers, 2002.

A comprehensive color resource for quilters! Includes practical advice about applying color theory to quilt palettes.

Wolfrom, Joen, *Color Play: Easy Steps to Imaginative Color in Quilts*. Lafayette, CA: C&T Publishing, 2000.

From soup to nuts about color with quilters in mind.

Wolfrom, Joen, *Visual Coloring: A Foolproof Approach to Color-Rich Quilts*. Lafayette, CA: C&T Publishing, 2007.

Another book on color for quilters from color expert Joen Wolfrom.

Wolfrom, Joen, Studio Color Wheel. Lafayette, CA: C&T Publishing, 2010.

A poster-size color wheel for your studio, based on Joen's Ultimate 3-in-1 Color Tool.

Wolfrom, Joen, Ultimate 3-in-1 Color Tool, Updated 3rd Edition. Lafayette, CA: C&T Publishing, 2010.

A pocket-size reference tool on color.

## Online Fabric Resources

**Blue Underground Studios, Inc.**
www.blueundergroundstudios.com
Our website! Check us out for unique kits, including many silks and solids.

**QuiltHome.com**
www.quilthome.com
QuiltHome carries a variety of contemporary quilting fabrics. Their website is user friendly and their service is outstanding.

**Glorious Color**
www.gloriouscolor.com
Great source for Westminster prints, including those designed by Kaffe Fassett, Philip Jacobs, and Brandon Mably.

**Fabricworm**
www.fabricworm.com
Fresh, modern fabric for the person devoted to fabric.

**Hancock's of Paducah**
www.hancocks-paducah.com
A great one-stop shop for a multitude of fabric lines. Also a great place to shop for batiks and solids.

**Fabric Shack**
www.fabricshack.com
A good resource for precut strip bundles, fat quarter packs, and batiks.

## Online Product Resource

**Dharma Trading Company**
www.dharmatrading.com
For Retayne (by G&K Craft Industries) and other supplies.

*Photo by Lisa Altmeyer / Black and White photography*

## Amy Walsh

Amy has been sewing and quilting ever since she was old enough to sit at the sewing machine. As a little girl, she used to sneak down the stairs after bedtime to spy on her mother's sewing bees. She started her fabric collection at an early age by storing it in her bedroom closet.

Throughout her years of college and teaching, sewing, and especially fabric, remained her passion. In 2004, Amy left her job teaching history and started working as a longarm quilter. Amy started Blue Underground Studios, Inc., with fellow longarm quilter Janine Burke in 2005.

Amy resides in Chicago with her husband and daughter.

## Janine Burke

Janine's grandmother taught her to sew while she was in grade school. She spent many hours embroidering dishtowels and pillowcases. Eventually her love of stitching led to a love of quilting, and she started collecting fabrics. After many years as a hobby quilter, Janine turned quilting into a career when she started longarm quilting. In addition to pattern design, she also teaches classes and works in the industry in several different capacities. Janine resides in the Chicago area.

# Great Titles and Products *from* C&T PUBLISHING

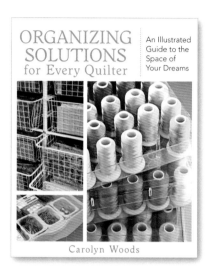

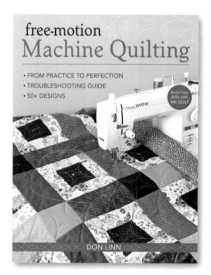

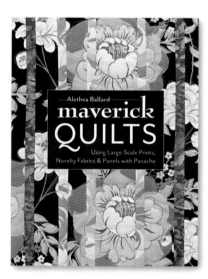

*Available at your local retailer or* **www.ctpub.com** *or* **800-284-1114**

For a list of other fine books from C&T Publishing, visit our website to view our catalog online.

**C&T PUBLISHING, INC.**

P.O. Box 1456
Lafayette, CA 94549
800-284-1114

Email: ctinfo@ctpub.com
Website: www.ctpub.com

C&T Publishing's professional photography services are now available to the public. Visit us at www.ctmediaservices.com.

**Tips and Techniques** can be found at www.ctpub.com > Consumer Resources > Quiltmaking Basics: Tips & Techniques for Quiltmaking & More

For quilting supplies:

**COTTON PATCH**

1025 Brown Ave.
Lafayette, CA 94549
Store: 925-284-1177
Mail order: 925-283-7883

Email: CottonPa@aol.com
Website: www.quiltusa.com

Note: Fabrics used in the quilts shown may not be currently available, as fabric manufacturers keep most fabrics in print for only a short time.